D0886631

LIVING THROUGH 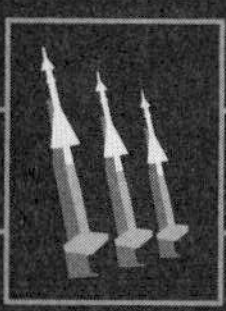 THE COLD WAR

LIVING THROUGH THE CUBAN MISSILE CRISIS

LIVING THROUGH  THE COLD WAR

LIVING THROUGH THE CUBAN MISSILE CRISIS

Other books in this series:

Living Through the End of the Cold War

Living Through the Vietnam War

Living Under the Threat of Nuclear War

LIVING THROUGH THE COLD WAR

LIVING THROUGH THE CUBAN MISSILE CRISIS

Edited by William S. McConnell

Bruce Glassman, *Vice President*
Bonnie Szumski, *Publisher*
Helen Cothran, *Managing Editor*
Scott Barbour, *Series Editor*

GREENHAVEN PRESS
An imprint of Thomson Gale, a part of The Thomson Corporation

Detroit • New York • San Francisco • San Diego • New Haven, Conn.
Waterville, Maine • London • Munich

For more information, contact
Greenhaven Press
27500 Drake Rd.
Farmington Hills, MI 48331-3535
Or you can visit our Internet site at http://www.gale.com

Cover credit: © Hulton-Deutsch Collection/CORBIS. Cuban soldiers demonstrate coastal defense artillery they used during the Bay of Pigs invasion in 1961.
John F. Kennedy Library, 79
Library of Congress, 17, 27, 44, 52, 112

LIBRARY OF CONGRESS CATALOGING-IN-PUBLICATION DATA

Living through the Cuban missile crisis / William S. McConnell, book editor.
p. cm. — (Living through the Cold War)
Includes bibliographical references and index.
ISBN 0-7377-2128-6 (lib. : alk. paper)
1. Cuban missile crisis, 1962. 2. Cuban missile crisis, 1962—Sources.
I. McConnell, William S. II. Series.

E841.C844 2005
972.9106'4—dc22 2004047476

Printed in the United States of America

CONTENTS

Chapter 2: Thirteen Days in October: The Crisis Unfolds

Chapter 3: Perspectives on the Crisis

At the midpoint of the Cold War, in early 1968, U.S. television viewers saw surprising reports from Vietnam, where American ground troops had been fighting since 1965. They learned that South Vietnamese Communist rebels, known as the Vietcong, had attacked unexpectedly throughout the country. At one point Vietcong insurgents engaged U.S. troops and officials in a firefight at the very center of U.S. power in Vietnam, the American embassy in South Vietnam's capital, Saigon. Meanwhile, thousands of soldiers and marines faced a concerted siege at Khe Sanh, an isolated base high in central Vietnam's mountains. Their adversary was not the Vietcong, but rather the regular North Vietnamese army.

Reporters and U.S. citizens quickly learned that these events constituted the Tet Offensive, a coordinated attack by Vietnamese Communists that occurred in late January, the period of Tet, Vietnam's new year. The American public was surprised by the Tet Offensive because they had been led to believe that the United States and its South Vietnamese allies were winning the war, that Vietcong forces were weak and dwindling, and that the massive buildup of American forces (there were some five hundred thousand U.S. troops in Vietnam by early 1968), ensured that the south would remain free of a Communist takeover. Since 1965, politicians, pundits, and generals had claimed that massive American intervention was justified and that the war was being won. On a publicity tour in November 1967 General William Westmoreland, the American commander in Vietnam, had assured officials and reporters that "the ranks of the Vietcong are thinning steadily" and that "we have reached a point where the end begins to come into view." President Lyndon B. Johnson's advisers, meanwhile, continually encouraged him to publicly emphasize "the light at the end of the tunnel."

Ordinary Americans had largely supported the troop buildup in Vietnam, believing the argument that the country was an important front in the Cold War, the global effort to stop the spread of communism that had begun in the late 1940s. Communist regimes already held power in nearby China, North Korea, and in northern Vietnam; it was deemed necessary to hold the line in the south not only to prevent communism from taking hold there but to prevent other nations from falling to communism throughout Asia. In 1965, polls showed that 80 percent of Americans believed that intervention in Vietnam was justified despite the fact that involvement in this fight would alter American life in numerous ways. For example, young men faced the possibility of being drafted and sent to fight—and possibly die—in a war thousands of miles away. As the war progressed, citizens watched more and more of their sons—both draftees and enlisted men—being returned to the United States in coffins (approximately fifty-eight thousand Americans died in Vietnam). Antiwar protests roiled college campuses and sometimes the streets of major cities. The material costs of the war threatened domestic political reforms and America's economic health, offering the continuing specter of rising taxes and shrinking services. Nevertheless, as long as the fight was succeeding, a majority of Americans could accept these risks and sacrifices.

Tet changed many minds, suggesting as it did that the war was not, in fact, going well. When CBS news anchor Walter Cronkite, who was known as "the most trusted man in America," suggested in his broadcast on the evening of February 27 that the Vietnam War might be unwinnable and could only end in a stalemate, many people wondered if he might be right and began to suspect that the positive reports from generals and politicians might have been misleading. It was a turning point in the battle for public opinion. Johnson reportedly said that Cronkite's expressions of doubt signaled the loss of mainstream America's support for the war. Indeed, after Tet more and more people joined Cronkite in wondering whether fighting this obscure enemy in an isolated country halfway around the world was worth the cost—whether it was a truly important front in the Cold War. They made their views known through demonstrations and opinion polls, and politicians were forced to respond. In a dramatic and unexpected turn of events, Johnson declined to run for reelection in 1968, stating that his involvement in the political campaign would detract from his efforts to negotiate a peace agreement with North Vietnam. His successor, Richard Nixon, won the election after promising to end the war.

The Tet Offensive and its consequences provide strong examples of how the Cold War touched the lives of ordinary Americans. Far from being an abstract geopolitical event, the Cold War, as Tet reveals, was an ever-present influence in the everyday life of the nation. Greenhaven Press's Living Through the Cold War series provides snapshots into the lives of ordinary people during the Cold War, as well as their reactions to its major events and developments. Each volume is organized around a particular event or distinct stage of the Cold War. Primary documents such as eyewitness accounts and speeches give firsthand insights into both ordinary peoples' experiences and leaders' decisions. Secondary sources provide factual information and place events within a larger global and historical context. Additional resources include a detailed introduction, a comprehensive chronology, and a thorough bibliography. Also included are an annotated table of contents and a detailed index to help the reader locate information quickly. With these features, the Living Through the Cold War series reveals the human dimension of the superpower rivalry that defined the globe during most of the latter half of the twentieth century.

INTRODUCTION

The Soviet Union maintained a military expansionist policy during the Cold War. Immediately following World War II, for example, the Soviet Union successfully took advantage of its weakened neighbors by invading several Eastern European countries through aggressive military action, creating a buffer of Communist countries along its western border. When the Soviets pushed into more territories, the United States and other nations chose to respond with political pressure instead of military force for fear of causing another world war. In 1962 Soviet premier Nikita Khrushchev, emboldened by the lack of intervention from other nations, attempted to expand the Soviet military presence into the Western Hemisphere and challenged the United States directly by installing nuclear missile silos in Cuba, a country just ninety miles from the coast of Florida.

Until the Cuban revolution of 1959, no Communist country had existed so close to the borders of the United States, and in October 1962, with the installation of Soviet missile silos in Cuba, the imminent threat of nuclear war had never seemed so near to home. These missile silos, if allowed to become fully operational, would have been able to launch a nuclear warhead to any point within the United States.

Nuclear threats were not new to the United States. Such threats had lingered over the globe since the Soviet Union had become a nuclear power. In fact, during the Eisenhower era, between 1953 and 1961, U.S. citizens prepared themselves for nuclear attacks by performing duck-and-cover drills in local schools and community centers. Americans were told that suitable shelter would provide adequate protection against nuclear attack and constructed thousands of backyard bomb shelters during the 1950s. Nevertheless, the sudden onset of the Cuban threat induced a new sense of fear that left many in the United States feeling helpless and panicked. During the thirteen days of the missile crisis, many people stockpiled goods such as canned water and dehydrated food. People panicked and sought out neighbors who had bomb shelters in an effort to secure protection for themselves and their families. Local governments established emergency shelters in schools and churches. Measures were taken to protect national treasures and priceless works of art. In those days of October 16 through October 28, 1962, the discovery of the missiles and the tense showdown that followed became not only a political confrontation between two superpowers, but an intense reality check about the possibility of an all-out nuclear war. The potential for such a confrontation had existed for over a decade, but the Cuban missile crisis brought the threat home and gave it a new sense of immediacy.

Uncovering the Threat

On October 14, 1962, a U-2 reconnaissance plane photographed the first evidence of nuclear-missile-silo construction in Cuba. The photographs also revealed the presence of nuclear missiles still in their crates and ready to be assembled for immediate use. On October 16 further reconnaissance flights revealed the presence of two types of missiles: medium-range ballistic missiles (MRBMs) that can reach a distance of thirteen hundred miles and intermediate-range ballistic missiles (IRBMs) that can reach a distance of twenty-five hundred miles. These missiles gave the Soviets the ability to strike at any major target within the United States and severely limit the ability of the United States to issue a nuclear response of its own.

In the days between October 16 and October 22, President John F. Kennedy met with his political and military advisers. Members of the White House staff contacted the Organization of American States (OAS), an assembly of Latin American countries. Kennedy's representatives informed the OAS governing body of the developments in Cuba. The OAS subsequently voted to "take all measures . . . including the use of armed force to prevent the missiles . . . from ever becoming a threat to the peace and security of the continents."[1] With the

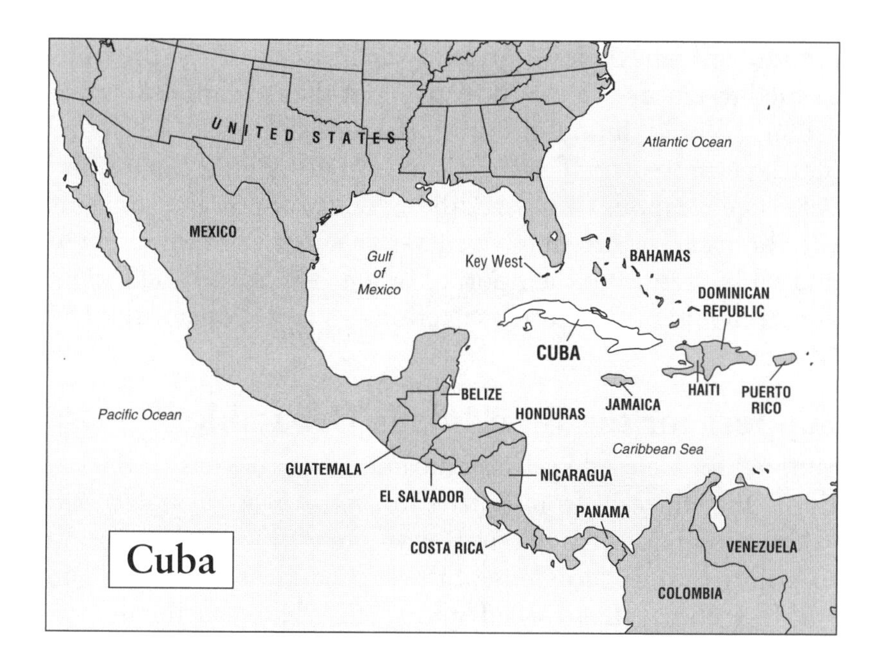

support of the entire Western Hemisphere behind him, Kennedy chose to inform the people of the United States and the nations of the world about the unfolding crisis in the Caribbean.

The President Declares a Naval Blockade of Cuba

On October 22, 1962, Kennedy addressed the nation and assured the people of the United States that the Cuban missile threat would not be allowed to continue. Kennedy believed that the first step to ending the crisis was halting the influx of weapons into Cuba. He stated that a naval blockade of the country would be put into place inspecting all ship traffic into Cuba for nuclear weapons. Furthermore, Kennedy pledged to retaliate against the Soviet Union if a nuclear missile was fired from Cuba at any nation in the Western Hemisphere. The president also vowed to sink any ships that attempted to break through the blockade without an inspection.

The naval blockade went into effect the next day, and on October 24 it was challenged for the first time. Several ships large enough to carry nuclear weapons were warned to turn around and halt their progress toward Cuba. At first the ships seemed to ignore the U.S. directive, but they eventually turned around. Not all inbound ship traffic was stopped. The United States permitted smaller ships carrying nonmilitary items and defensive weapons to pass. Although only one Soviet ship was ever boarded, more than twenty-five ships were intercepted and told to return to their port of origin. The Soviet and Cuban governments protested these actions as violations of the UN Charter.

Support for the Blockade Is Debatable

Support for Kennedy's decision came from all parts of the nation. One editorial from *Seattle Journal American* stated that "the action had to be taken. It was a magnificent declaration of policy that acknowledged the risks an unscrupulous and ruthless enemy has forced upon us."[2] This sentiment was echoed in small and major market newspapers throughout the United States. In Hartford, Connecticut, commentary from the local newspaper *Courant* stated, "The blockade is war, if anyone chooses to challenge our blockade. It is up to Mr. Khrushchev. Let him reflect before he acts. Let him not misread the mood of America or misjudge her as Kaiser [Frederick] Wilhelm [the leader of Germany during World War I] and Adolf Hitler [the leader of Germany during World War II] did to let loose two world wars."[3] Finally, in Chicago's *Sun Times*, one commentator remarked that "President Kennedy has spoken the mind and the fear of his fellow Americans. Come what may, the people of this country will back Mr. Kennedy."[4]

Although these were bold statements reflecting a unified atmosphere of support behind Kennedy's naval blockade, not all Americans were behind the decision. Harvard University professor H. Stuart Hughes used the crisis in his effort to build up Harvard's peace movement program, one of many such university-based organizations that would become prominent in the effort to end the Vietnam War in the latter half of the 1960s. Hughes, who was running as an independent for the Massachusetts state senate, telegraphed copies of his peace proposals to several world leaders, including Kennedy, secretary-general of the

Members of an antiwar organization protest outside of the White House in October 1962, in response to U.S. accusations against Cuba.

United Nations U Thant, UN ambassador Adlai Stevenson, and Soviet premier Khrushchev. Hughes's papers implored the world leaders for peace. Even though he attempted to contact world leaders, Hughes's message was directed mostly at students in the hope that they could organize a vocal presence against the possibility of war, but as *New York Times* journalist John Fenton wrote, Hughes's message "had little impact on students in the Boston area beyond Harvard Square."[5]

Similar protests occurred in Canada. Students from several universities in Montreal organized demonstrations in front of the U.S. Consulate and demanded that the United States stop interfering in the domestic affairs of Cuba and other nations. Not all protests were peaceful. In Moscow the car carrying U.S. ambassador Foy D. Kohler was hit with a stone, although Kohler escaped unharmed. Similar reports of minor violence, most of which focused on U.S. embassies, occurred in Copenhagen, Budapest, London, and Sydney. Although protests like these were not widespread, they did reveal a burgeoning vocal presence that stood against military confrontations between nations.

Americans Feel Unprepared to Safeguard Communities

Although Kennedy and Khrushchev worked behind closed doors to resolve the crisis without a war, the rest of the United States remained tense. The American Civil Defense Commission had been arduous in its duties throughout the 1950s in preparing local governments for war. Air sirens had been installed in some areas to warn of a missile launch. Some local bomb shelters had been established, and duck-and-cover drills were held for children so that they might feel safe in a nuclear attack. But none of these actions prepared Americans for the reality of a nuclear war, leaving many Americans frightened about the possible outcome of the crisis. To help citizens feel safe, communities quickly reviewed their emergency response policies and began to organize safety measures. Communities designated town halls, churches, and YMCA buildings as emergency shelters in the event of a war.

In a recent BBC News report, several Americans gave detailed accounts of how they felt at this time. One young woman recalled, "I was only six years old . . . however my brother, who was eight at the time, was terrified. My sisters remember him praying on his knees at his bedside that we would not have a nuclear war. What a horrible thing for a little boy to go through." Others expected missiles to fall out of the sky at any moment. A man who was a teenager at the time recalls, "I was expecting a bright flash in the sky or horizon, day after day spelling the end of the earth for us all." And finally, another American recalls "seeing anxiety and fear in people. I remember the media showing people building shelters in their backyards, and I recollect seeing grocery stores being almost devoid of certain food items. Upon seeing this hoarding of food, it hit me that a nuclear war was indeed a very high possibility, and that truly scared me."[6] Even in Cuba, children were taught to hide in the event of a nuclear attack or an invasion by U.S. soldiers. In an interview with CNN reporter Lucia Newman, one Cuban national, Maria Leiva, states that she remembers being taught that "if you are sleeping and there is an invasion, you have to run to where you already know you have to run. Here everyone in the country knows where they have to go [to be safe]."[7] Overall, Americans and others throughout the globe continued feeling helpless while they waited for Kennedy to reach a suitable agreement with Khrushchev.

Reaching a Resolution

Between October 26 and October 28, Kennedy and Khrushchev exchanged top secret telegrams. Each leader offered the other a peace proposal. Khrushchev wanted Kennedy to remove U.S. missiles in Turkey along the southern border of the Soviet Union in exchange for removing the missiles in Cuba. The missile silos in Turkey were viewed as obsolete by U.S. military advisers, and Kennedy even felt that the public would support their withdrawal. However, Kennedy's advisers warned against removing the missiles in response to a Soviet demand. Instead, Kennedy decided to publicly announce that he would accept a Soviet offer to remove the missiles in Cuba in exchange for a promise that America would not invade the island nation. Privately, Kennedy sent his brother, U.S. attorney general Robert F. Kennedy, to the Soviet embassy in New York to assure Soviet ambassador Anatoly Dobrynin that the missiles in Turkey would be removed when the missile silos in Cuba were dismantled and shipped back to the Soviet Union.

On October 28 the tension began to diminish. Fearing that a nuclear war was inevitable, Khrushchev accepted Kennedy's offer. In a public radio address, Khrushchev said he would remove offensive weapons from Cuba and requested the aid of UN inspectors to assist with the removal process. Castro still believed that the United States intended to invade his country. He refused to permit the UN to inspect the missile sites. He even went as far as to urge Khrushchev to launch the missiles. To help reassure Castro, UN secretary-general U Thant traveled to Cuba and agreed on a time line for inspectors to come and verify that the missile silos were dismantled. Castro and Thant decided that all Soviet bombers would be crated and shipped back to the Soviet Union within thirty days, and the missiles would be dismantled in the open, allowing U.S. surveillance aircraft to observe the process.

Emerging from the Crisis

The crisis ended, leaving many to hail Kennedy's efforts as heroic. The peaceful resolution to the crisis enhanced the global view of the United States as a country that was willing to do more than just negotiate with Communists through political tactics. The direct confrontation of the Soviet Union through the naval blockade gave the United States credibility as an adversary that would not allow itself to be taken advantage of in the future. According to *Christian Science Monitor* news correspondent Richard L. Stout, "The United States's credibility, in the language of the cold war, would have been long in doubt"[8] had Kennedy chosen not to use a military intervention in response to this direct threat of nuclear war. The resolution, though, did nothing to stop the Cold War. Although both superpowers stood down from a nuclear war, both nations continued to build up their arsenals of nuclear missiles at an increasing pace in the years to come.

The withdrawal of the Soviets from Cuba also did nothing to solve other conflicts with communism throughout the globe. The Communist control of East Berlin was still a volatile political issue between the United States and the Soviet Union. The United States was also becoming more steadily involved in Vietnam. The Cuban crisis influenced the United States to take a stricter stance against communism in these areas, especially in Vietnam. And although the president had the support of the nation behind him during this crisis, Americans became increasingly opposed to U.S. intervention in other areas of the globe where communism was a factor. After the crisis was resolved, Americans also realized how unprotected they were against nuclear attacks. Duck-and-cover drills helped children to feel safe in schools, but they provided no real protection in the event of an actual nuclear attack. Fallout shelters also became less popular as more people understood the dangers of radiation exposure and nuclear fallout. The idea that one could be confined to such a small space with only a one- or two-month's supply of food seemed impractical as knowledge increased about the aftereffects of a nuclear war.

The United States may have seemed unified after the crisis, but many more people were skeptical of the road ahead. The call for nuclear disarmament increased through student activities and demonstrations. Many people came to believe that the best defense against a nuclear war was to ban nuclear weapons. The Cuban missile crisis compelled the United States, Great Britain, and the Soviet Union to sign in 1963 the Limited Nuclear Test Ban Treaty, which outlawed nuclear test detonations in the air or the ocean but allowed them underground.

The Cuban missile crisis was perhaps the most influential test of the Cold War. In many ways the United States passed the test and achieved its peaceful victory over the Soviet Union. But the U.S. policy to stop the spread of communism throughout the globe was only inflamed by the crisis and encouraged the United States to intervene against communism in future years, even in the face of defeat.

Notes

1. Quoted in the *New York Times*, "The News of the Week in Review," October 28, 1962.
2. *Seattle Journal American*, "In the Name of Courage," as quoted in "Excerpts from Newspaper Editorials on Decision to Blockade Cuba," *New York Times*, October 24, 1962.
3. *Hartford Courant*, "Up to Khrushchev," as quoted in "Excerpts from Newspaper Editorials on Decision to Blockade Cuba," *New York Times*, October 24, 1962.
4. *Chicago Sun Times*, "Patience at an End," as quoted in "Excerpts from Newspaper Editorials on Decision to Blockade Cuba," *New York Times*, October 24, 1962.
5. John H. Fenton, "Campuses Voice Some Opposition," *New York Times*, October 25, 1962.
6. Quoted in BBC News: Talking Point, "Missile Crisis: Your Memories." http://news.bbc.co.uk/1/hi/world/Americas/2317931.stm.
7. Quoted in Lucia Newman, "Cold War Continues in Cuba." www.cnn.com/SPECIALS/cold.war/episodes/10/then.now.
8. Richard L. Stout, "Why Crisis Flared Up," *Christian Science Monitor*, October 25, 1962.

CHAPTER 1

Official Statements on the Crisis

President Kennedy Addresses the Nation

John F. Kennedy

On October 16, 1962, a U.S. air reconnaissance flight over Cuba revealed that the Soviet Union was in the process of installing nuclear missiles on that island nation. In the days following this discovery, President John F. Kennedy counseled with the Soviet representative in the United States, Andrei Gromyko, who assured Kennedy that the weapons were not offensive first-strike nuclear weapons, but defensive weapons that would help protect the sovereignty of Cuba in the event of a U.S. invasion. President Kennedy then met with key members of his cabinet, including top military personnel, to further study the reconnaissance photos and discuss possible response options. After deciding that the weapons in the photos were offensive nuclear missiles, Kennedy and his advisers decided to quarantine Cuba with a naval blockade to prevent any further shipments of nuclear arms into the country until a resolution to this mounting crisis could be reached. In this speech, delivered to an American television audience on October 22, 1962, President Kennedy states that the placement of nuclear missiles in Cuba is a threat to national security and a threat to the Western Hemisphere, and he demands the immediate removal of these weapons from Cuba.

This Government, as promised, has maintained the closest surveillance of the Soviet Military buildup on the island of

John F. Kennedy, televised address to the nation, Washington, DC, October 22, 1962.

Cuba. Within the past week, unmistakable evidence has established the fact that a series of offensive missile sites is now in preparation on that imprisoned island. The purpose of these bases can be none other than to provide a nuclear strike capability against the Western Hemisphere.

Upon receiving the first preliminary hard information of this nature last Tuesday [October 16, 1962] morning at 9 A.M., I directed that our surveillance be stepped up. And having now confirmed and completed our evaluation of the evidence and our decision on a course of action, this Government feels obliged to report this new crisis to you in fullest detail.

Informing the Public of the Nuclear Threat

The characteristics of these new missile sites indicate two distinct types of installations. Several of them include medium range ballistic missiles capable of carrying a nuclear warhead for a distance of more than 1,000 nautical miles. Each of these missiles, in short, is capable of striking Washington, D.C., the Panama Canal, Cape Canaveral, Mexico City, or any other city in the southeastern part of the United States, in Central America, or in the Caribbean area.

Additional sites not yet completed appear to be designed for intermediate range ballistic missiles—capable of traveling more than twice as far—and thus capable of striking most of the major cities in the Western Hemisphere, ranging as far north as Hudson Bay, Canada, and as far south as Lima, Peru. In addition, jet bombers, capable of carrying nuclear weapons, are now being uncrated and assembled in Cuba, while the necessary air bases are being prepared. . . .

The size of this undertaking makes clear that it has been planned for some months. Yet only last month, after I had made clear the distinction between any introduction of ground-to-ground missiles and the existence of defensive antiaircraft missiles, the Soviet Government publicly stated on September 11, and I quote, "the armaments and military equipment sent to Cuba are designed exclusively for defensive purposes," that, and I quote the Soviet Government, "there is no need for the Soviet Government to shift its weapons . . . for a retaliatory blow to any other country, for instance Cuba," and that, and I quote their government, "the Soviet Union has so powerful rockets to carry these nuclear warheads that there is no need to search for sites for them beyond the boundaries of the Soviet Union." That statement was false.

Only last Thursday [September 18, 1962], as evidence of this rapid offensive buildup was already in my hand, Soviet Foreign Minister Gromyko told me in my office that he was instructed to make it clear once again, as he said his government had already done, that Soviet assistance to Cuba, and I quote, "pursued solely the purpose of contributing to the defense capabilities of Cuba," that, and I quote him, "training by Soviet specialists of Cuban nationals in handling defensive armaments was by no means offensive, and if it were otherwise," Mr. Gromyko went on, "the Soviet Government would never become involved in rendering such assistance." That statement also was false.

A Clear and Present Danger

Neither the United States of America nor the world community of nations can tolerate deliberate deception and offensive threats on the part of any nation, large or small. We no longer live in a world where only the actual firing of weapons represents a sufficient challenge to a nation's security to constitute maximum peril. Nuclear weapons are so destructive and ballistic missiles are so swift, that any substantially increased possibility of their use or any sudden change in their deployment may well be regarded as a definite threat to peace.

For many years both the Soviet Union and the United States, recognizing this fact, have deployed strategic nuclear weapons with great care, never upsetting the precarious status quo which insured that these weapons would not be used in the absence of some vital challenge. Our own strategic missiles have never been transferred to the territory of any other nation under a cloak of secrecy and deception; and our history—unlike that of the Soviets since the end of World War II—demonstrates that we have no desire to dominate or conquer any other nation or impose our system upon its people.

Nevertheless, American citizens have become adjusted to living daily on the Bull's-eye of Soviet missiles located inside the U.S.S.R. or in submarines.

In that sense, missiles in Cuba add to an already clear and present danger—although it should be noted the nations of Latin America have never previously been subjected to a potential nuclear threat.

But this secret, swift, and extraordinary buildup of Communist missiles—in an area well known to have a special and historical relationship to the United States and the nations of the Western Hemisphere, in violation of Soviet assurances, and in defiance of American and hemispheric policy—this sudden, clandestine decision to station strategic weapons for the first time outside of Soviet soil—is a deliberately provocative and unjustified change in the status quo which cannot be accepted by this country, if our courage and our commitments are ever to be trusted again by either friend or foe.

The 1930's taught us a clear lesson: aggressive conduct, if allowed to go unchecked and unchallenged ultimately leads to war. This nation is opposed to war. We are also true to our word. Our unswerving objective, therefore, must be to prevent the use of these missiles against this or any other country, and to secure their withdrawal or elimination from the Western Hemisphere.

Seven Steps to Combat the Crisis

Our policy has been one of patience and restraint, as befits a peaceful and powerful nation, which leads a worldwide alliance. We have been determined not to be diverted from our central concerns by mere irritants and fanatics. But now further action is required—and it is under way; and these actions may only be the beginning. We will not prematurely or unnecessarily risk the costs of worldwide nuclear war in which even the fruits of victory would be ashes in our mouth—but neither will we shrink from that risk at any time it must be faced.

Acting, therefore, in the defense of our own security and of the entire Western Hemisphere, and under the authority entrusted to me by the Constitution as endorsed by the resolution of the Congress, I have directed that the following initial steps be taken immediately:

First: To halt this offensive buildup, a strict quarantine on all offensive military equipment under shipment to Cuba is being initiated. All ships of any kind bound for Cuba from whatever nation or port will, if found to contain cargoes of offensive weapons, be turned back. This quarantine will be extended, if needed, to other types of cargo and carriers. We are not at this time, however, denying the necessities of life as the Soviets attempted to do in their Berlin blockade of 1948. [The Soviet Union stopped all imports, forcing the United States and Great Britain to air drop supplies into the city.]

Second: I have directed the continued and increased close surveillance of Cuba and its military buildup. The foreign ministers of the OAS [Organization of American States], in their communique of October 6 [1962], rejected secrecy in such

Cuban refugees listen to President Kennedy's announcement that the Soviet Union was installing nuclear missiles in Cuba.

matters in this hemisphere. Should these offensive military preparations continue, thus increasing the threat to the hemisphere, further action will be justified. I have directed the Armed Forces to prepare for any eventualities; and I trust that in the interest of both the Cuban people and the Soviet technicians at the sites, the hazards to all concerned in continuing this threat will be recognized.

Third: It shall be the policy of this Nation to regard any nuclear missile launched from Cuba against any nation in the Western Hemisphere as an attack by the Soviet Union on the United States, requiring a full retaliatory response upon the Soviet Union.

Fourth: As a necessary military precaution, I have reinforced our base at Guantanamo [U.S. Naval base located at the north end of Cuba], evacuated today the dependents of our personnel there, and ordered additional military units to be on a standby alert basis.

Fifth: We are calling tonight for an immediate meeting of the Organ of Consultation [the governing body of OAS] under the Organization of American States, to consider this threat to hemispheric security and to invoke articles 6 and 8 of the Rio Treaty [treaty of reciprocal assistance between Nations of the Western Hemisphere] in support of all necessary action. The United Nations Charter allows for regional security arrangements—and the nations of this hemisphere decided long ago against the military presence of outside powers. Our other allies around the world have also been alerted.

Sixth: Under the Charter of the United Nations, we are asking tonight that an emergency meeting of the Security Council be convoked without delay to take action against this latest Soviet threat to world peace. Our resolution will call for the prompt dismantling and withdrawal of all offensive weapons in Cuba, under the supervision of U.N. observers, before the quarantine can be lifted.

Seventh and finally: I call upon [Soviet] Chairman [Nikita] Khrushchev to halt and eliminate this clandestine, reckless and provocative threat to world peace and to stable relations between our two nations. I call upon him further to abandon this course of world domination, and to join in an historic effort to end the perilous arms race and to transform the history of man. He has an opportunity now to move the world back from the abyss of destruction—by returning to his government's own words that it had no need to station missiles outside its own territory, and withdrawing these weapons from Cuba—by refraining from any action which will widen or deepen the present crisis—and then by participating in a search for peaceful and permanent solutions.

A Commitment to Peace

This Nation is prepared to present its case against the Soviet threat to peace, and our own proposals for a peaceful world, at any time and in any forum—in the OAS, in the United Nations, or in any other meeting that could be useful—without limiting our freedom of action. We have in the past made strenuous efforts to limit the spread of nuclear weapons. We have proposed the elimination of all arms and military bases in a fair and effective disarmament treaty. We are prepared to discuss new proposals for the removal of tensions on both sides—including the possibility of a genuinely independent Cuba, free to determine its own destiny. We have no wish to war with the Soviet Union—for we are a peaceful people who desire to live in peace with all other peoples.

But it is difficult to settle or even discuss these problems in an atmosphere of intimidation. That is why this latest Soviet threat—or any other threat which is made independently or in response to our actions this week—must and will be met with determination. Any hostile move anywhere in the world against the safety and freedom of peoples to whom we are committed—including in particular the brave people of West Berlin—will be met by whatever action is needed.

A Plea to the Cuban People

Finally, I want to say a few words to the captive people of Cuba, to whom this speech is being directly carried by special radio facilities. I speak to you as a friend, as one who knows of your deep attachment to your fatherland, as one who shares your aspirations for liberty and justice for all. And I have watched and the American people have watched with deep sorrow how your nationalist revolution was betrayed—and how your fatherland fell under foreign domination. Now your leaders are no longer Cuban leaders inspired by Cuban ideals. They are puppets and agents of an international conspiracy which has turned Cuba against your friends and neighbors in the Americas—and turned it into the first Latin American country to become a target for nuclear war—the first Latin American country to have these weapons on its soil.

These new weapons are not in your interest. They contribute nothing to your peace and well-being. They can only undermine it. But this country has no wish to cause you to suffer or to impose any system upon you. We know that your lives and land are being used as pawns by those who deny your freedom.

Many times in the past, the Cuban people have risen to throw out tyrants who destroyed their liberty. And I have no doubt that most Cubans today look forward to the time when they will be truly free—free from foreign domination, free to choose their own leaders, free to select their own system, free to own their own land, free to speak and write and worship without fear or degradation. And then shall Cuba be welcomed back to the society of free nations and to the associations of this hemisphere.

An Unsure Future

My fellow citizens: let no one doubt that this is a difficult and dangerous effort on which we have set out. No one can see precisely what course it will take or what costs or casualties will be incurred. Many months of sacrifice and self-discipline lie ahead—months in which our patience and our will will be tested—months in which many threats and denunciations will keep us aware of our dangers. But the greatest danger of all would be to do nothing.

The path we have chosen for the present is full of hazards, as all paths are—but it is the one most consistent with our character and courage as a nation and our commitments around the world. The cost of freedom is always high—and Americans have always paid it. And one path we shall never choose, and that is the path of surrender or submission.

Our goal is not the victory of might, but the vindication of right—not peace at the expense of freedom, but both peace and freedom, here in this hemisphere, and, we hope, around the world. God willing, that goal will be achieved.

Debating the Existence of Nuclear Missiles in Cuba

Adlai Stevenson and Valerian Zorin

On October 23, 1962, Adlai Stevenson and Valerian Zorin debated the issue of nuclear weapons in Cuba. This debate, as follows, is presented in two parts. Part one is the U.S. case presented by Adlai Stevenson, who served as U.S. ambassador from 1961 until his death in 1965. Part two of the debate is presented by the Soviet ambassador Valerian Zorin, who held several important positions within the Soviet Union during its armed takeover of Eastern European countries such as Czechoslovakia and Hungary. In his testimony, Stevenson argues that Cuba's willingness to allow the Soviet Union to establish offensive nuclear missile bases in the Western Hemisphere is an example of the Soviet Union's aggressive expansion campaign in the Americas. He tells the Security Council that the United States will go forward with its naval quarantine of Cuba in an effort to prevent any such expansion in the Western Hemisphere, as any threat to the Americas is considered a direct threat to the peace and security of the United States.

Zorin contends that the Soviet Union has shipped no nuclear missiles to Cuba. He argues that any weapons the Soviets have shipped are for defensive purposes only. Finally, he claims that the U.S. accusation is another example of U.S. aggression toward Cuba in an attempt to overthrow the Communist dictator Fidel Castro.

Adlai Stevenson and Valerian Zorin, statements before the United Nations Security Council, October 23, 1962.

Part I: Adlai Stevenson's Accusation

I have asked for an emergency meeting of the Security Council to bring to your attention a grave threat to the Western Hemisphere and to the peace of the world.

Last night, the President of the United States reported the recent alarming military developments in Cuba.

In view of this transformation of Cuba into a base for offensive weapons of sudden mass destruction, the President announced the initiation of a strict quarantine on all offensive military weapons under shipment to Cuba. He did so because, in the view of my Government, the recent developments in Cuba—the importation of the cold war into the heart of the Americas—constitute a threat to the peace of this hemisphere, and, indeed, to the peace of the world.

The time has come for this Council to decide whether to make a serious attempt to bring peace to the world—or to let the United Nations stand idly by while the vast plan of piecemeal aggression unfolds, conducted in the hope that no single issue will seem consequential enough to mobilize the resistance of the free peoples. For my own Government, this question is not in doubt. We remain committed to the principles of the United Nations, and we intend to defend them.

The Problem Revolves Around a Soviet Presence

Let me make it absolutely clear what the issue of Cuba is. It is not an issue of revolution. This hemisphere has seen many revolutions, including the one which gave my own nation its independence.

It is not an issue of reform. My nation has lived happily with other countries which have had thorough-going and fundamental social transformations, like Mexico and Bolivia. The whole point of the Alliance for Progress [President Kennedy's ten-point proposal for social and economic reform in Latin America] is to bring about an econonnc and social revolution in the Americas.

It is not an issue of socialism. As Secretary of State [Dean] Rusk said in February, "our hemisphere has room for a diversity of economic systems."

It is not an issue of dictatorship. The American Republics have lived with dictators before. If this were his only fault, they could live with Mr. Castro.

The foremost objection of the States of the Americas to the Castro régime is not because it is revolutionary, not because it is socialistic, not because it is dictatorial, not even because Mr. Castro perverted a noble revolution in the interests of a squalid totalitarianism. It is because he has aided and abetted an invasion of this hemisphere—an invasion just at the time when the hemisphere is making a new and unprecedented effort for economic progress and social reform.

The crucial fact is that Cuba has given the Soviet Union a bridgehead and staging area in this hemisphere; that it has invited an extra-continental, antidemocratic and expansionist Power into the bosom of the American family; that it has made itself an accomplice in the communist enterprise of world dominion.

The United States Must Intervene to Ensure Peace

In our passion for peace we have forborne greatly. There must, however, be limits to forbearance if forbearance is not to become the diagram for the destruction of this Organization. Mr. Castro transformed Cuba into a totalitarian dictatorship with impunity; he extinguished the rights of political freedom with impunity; he aligned himself with the Soviet bloc with impunity; he accepted defensive weapons from the Soviet Union with impunity; he welcomed thousands of Communists into Cuba with impunity: but when, with cold deliberation, he turns his country over to the Soviet Union for a long-range missile launching base, and thus carries the Soviet program for aggression into the heart of the Americas, the day of forbearance is past.

If the United States and the other nations of the Western Hemisphere should accept this new phase of aggression, we would be delinquent in our obligations to world peace. If the United States and the other nations of the Western Hemisphere should accept this basic disturbance of the world's structure of power we would invite a new surge of aggression at every point along the frontier. If we do not stand firm here our adversaries may think that we will stand firm nowhere—and guarantee a heightening of the world civil war to new levels of intensity and peril.

The issue which confronts the Security Council is grave. Were it not, I should not have detained you so long. Since the end of the Second World War, there has been no threat to the vision of peace so profound—no challenge to the world of the Charter so fateful. The hopes of mankind are concentrated in this room. The action we take may determine the future of civilization. I know that this Council will approach the issue with a full sense of our responsibility and a solemn understanding of the import of our deliberations.

There is a road to peace. The beginning of that road is marked out in the draft resolution I have submitted for your consideration. If we act promptly, we will have another chance to take up again the dreadful questions of nuclear arms and military bases and the means and causes of aggression and of war—to take them up and do something about them.

This is, I believe, a solemn and significant day for the life of the United Nations and the hope of the world community. Let it be remembered not as the day when the world came to the edge of nuclear war, but as the day when men resolved to let nothing thereafter stop them in their quest for peace.

Part II: Valerian Zorin's Rebuttal

I should now like to make a statement in my capacity as the representative of the Union of Soviet Socialist Republics.

I must say that even a cursory examination of Mr. Stevenson's statement reveals the totally untenable nature of the position taken by the United States Government on the question which it has thought necessary to place before the Council, amid its complete inability to defend this position in the Council and before world public opinion.

Mr. Stevenson touched on many subjects. . . . He spoke about the history of the Cuban revolution—although it is difficult to understand what the United States has to do with the internal affairs of the sovereign State of Cuba—and he drew an idyllic picture of the history of the Western Hemisphere for the past 150 years, seeming to forget about the policy of the "big stick" [a term used to describe the ascension of U.S. dominance as a moral imperative] followed by the United States President McKinley, the Olney Doctrine [established in 1895, this doctrine asserts the right of the United States to intervene in any international dispute impacting the Americas], the actions taken by Theodore Roosevelt in connexion with the Panama Canal, the boastful statement made by the American General Butler to the effect that with his marines he could hold elections in any Latin American country.

He made no mention of all this. The United States is even now attempting to apply this policy of the "big stick." But Mr. Stevenson apparently forgot that times have changed.

Accusing the United States of Ignoring International Law

Yesterday, the United States Government placed the Republic of Cuba under a virtual naval blockade. Insolently flouting the rules of international conduct and the principles of the Charter, the United States has arrogated to itself—and has so stated—the right to attack the ships of other States on the high seas, which is nothing less than undisguised piracy. At the same time, the landing of additional United States troops has begun at the United States Guantanamo base in Cuban territory, and the United States armed forces are being placed in a state of combat readiness.

The present aggressive actions of the United States of America against Cuba represent a logical stage in that aggressive policy, fraught with the most serious international consequences, which the United States began to pursue towards Cuba in the days of the Eisenhower Administration and which has been continued and intensified by the present United States Government, in the era of the "new frontier" that it proclaimed at the outset of its activities.

The United States Has a History of Aggression Toward Cuba

Everyone will remember Mr. Stevenson's statement on 15 April [1961] that the United States was not planning any aggression against Cuba, while on 17 April United States mercenaries landed at Playa Girón [refers to the Bay of Pigs invasion in which the United States backed and trained Cuban mercenaries to assassinate Fidel Castro]. What credence are we to attach to the statements of the representative of a great Power who dared to mislead world public opinion and the official organs of the United Nations in order to conceal the activities of the United States intelligence agency which was preparing for aggression and had ordered Mr. Stevenson to say nothing about it?

The falsity of the charges now levelled by the United States against the Soviet Union, which consist in the allegation that the Soviet Union has set offensive weapons in Cuba, is perfectly clear from the start. First of all, the Soviet delegation hereby officially confirms the statements already made by the Soviet Union in this connexion, to the effect that the Soviet Government has never sent and is not now sending offensive weapons of any kind to Cuba. The Soviet delegation would recall, in particular, the statement issued by [the official Russian news agency] Tass on 11 September of this year [1962] on the instructions of the Soviet Government, in which the following passage occurs:

The Government of the Soviet Union has authorized Tass to state, further, that the Soviet Union does not need to transfer to any other country, such as Cuba, its existing means for the repelling of aggression amid the delivering of a retaliatory blow. The explosive force of our nuclear resources is so great, and the Soviet Union has such powerful rockets for the delivery of these nuclear charges, that there is no need to seek places for their installation anywhere outside the borders of the Soviet Union.

The United States delegation is now trying to use its own fabrications in the Security Council for absolutely monstrous purposes—in order to try to obtain the retroactive approval of the Security Council of the illegal acts of aggression already undertaken by the United States against Cuba, acts which the United States is undertaking unilaterally and in manifest violation of the United Nations Charter and of the elementary rules amid principles of international law.

The peoples of the world must clearly realize, however, that in openly embarking on this venture the United States of America is taking a step along the road which leads to a thermonuclear world war. Such is the heavy price which the world may have to pay for the present reckless and irresponsible actions of the United States.

Peace-loving nations have long been afraid that the reckless aggressive policy of the United States with regard to Cuba may push the world to the brink of disaster. The alarm of the peace-loving elements and their efforts to induce the United States Government to listen to the voice of reason and accept a peaceful settlement of its differences with Cuba have been manifested in the course of the general debate during the seventeenth session of the General Assembly, which ended only a few days ago.

When it announced the introduction of its blockade against Cuba, the United States took a step which is unprecedented in relations between States not formally at war. By its arbitrary and piratical action, the United States menaced the shipping of many countries—including its allies—which do not agree with its reckless and dangerous policy in respect of Cuba. By this aggressive action, which put the whole world under the threat of war, the United States issued a direct challenge to the United Nations and to the Security Council as the principal organ of the United Nations responsible for maintaining international peace and security.

Laying Out the Soviet Case Against the United States

The Security Council would not be carrying out its bounden duty, as the principal organ responsible for maintaining world and international security, if it ignored the aggressive actions of the United States, which mean nothing less than that the United States has set out to destroy the United Nations and to unleash a world war.

What, then, are the actual facts now facing the Security Council? These facts may be summarized as follows:

(a) The United States Government has stated that it will take action against the ships of other countries, sailing on the high seas, of a type for which there can be no other name but piracy. The decision of the United States to stop and search

Cuba-bound ships of other countries will lead to an extreme heightening of international tension, and is a step towards provoking a thermonuclear world war, because no self-respecting State will permit its ships to be interfered with.

(b) In order to cover up its actions, the United States is putting forward pretexts which are made up out of whole cloth. It is trying to misrepresent the measures taken by the Cuban Government to ensure the defence of Cuba. Like any State which values its sovereignty and independence, Cuba can hardly fail to display serious anxiety for its security in the face of aggression.

(c) From the very first days of its existence, post-revolutionary Cuba has been subjected to continuous threats and provocation by the United States, which has stopped at nothing, including armed intervention in Cuba in April 1961.

(d) The United States imperialists have openly declared that they intend to impose their policies on other countries, and they are brazenly demanding that armaments intended for national defence should be removed from Cuban soil.

(e) The Soviet Government has consistently advocated that all foreign armed forces and armaments should be withdrawn from the territory of other countries to within their own national boundaries. This Soviet proposal is intended to clear the international atmosphere and set up conditions of mutual trust and understanding among nations. However, the United States Government, which has stationed its troops and military equipment all over the world, stubbornly refuses to accept this proposal of the Soviet Union. . . .

(f) The United States has no right whatever, either from the point of views of the accepted rules of international law relating to freedom of shipping, or from that of the provisions of the United Nations Charter, to put forward the demands contained in the statements of President Kennedy. No State, no matter how powerful it may be, has any right to rule on the quantities or types of arms which another State considers necessary for its defence. According to the United Nations Charter, each State has the right to defend itself and to possess weapons to ensure its security. . . .

(g) The attitude of the United States, as set forth in President Kennedy's statement, is a complete contradiction of the principles of the United Nations Charter and other generally accepted rules of international law. . . . The road which the United States is taking with regard to Cuba and the Soviet Union leads to the destruction of the United Nations and to the unleashing of war.

(h) The Soviet Government calls on all the peoples of the world to raise their voices in defence of the United Nations, to refuse to permit the break-up of this Organization, and to oppose the policy of piracy and thermonuclear warmongering followed by the United States. . . .

We call on all the members of the Security Council and—so serious is this question—even on the allies of the United Sates to weigh carefully, all the possible consequences of the present aggressive actions of the United States and to realize to what a disastrous course of action the United States is trying to commit the Security Council and the world as a whole. . . .

The realization by delegations of their responsibility for the outcome of the train of events set in motion by the aggressive actions of the United States against Cuba is, in the present situation, of direct significance not only for the settling of the present difficulties in the Caribbean, but also for the fate of peace throughout the world.

U.S. Accusations Are an Open Act of Aggression

Fidel Castro

From the onset of President John F. Kennedy's administration, Communist Cuba was the target of U.S. covert operatives plotting to overthrow Cuban dictator Fidel Castro in order to establish a democratic form of government in the tiny island nation. In 1961, in the most notable act of attempted intervention, the United States trained Cuban exiles in Florida and used them to launch an attack at Playa de Girón, also called the Bay of Pigs invasion. Castro, expecting a U.S.-led assault, reinforced the area with Cuban militia who, armed with Soviet weaponry, fought off the attack. The assault was a dismal failure and resulted in global embarrassment for the Kennedy administration. Due to further insinuations of U.S.-backed aggression toward Cuba, the Soviet Union proceeded to supply Castro with guns, planes, and other weapons necessary to confront the U.S. military. The United States was aware of the influx of weaponry into Cuba, but did not take action to prevent a buildup, choosing instead to follow a "wait and see" policy—a policy that contributed to the Soviets' ability to import nuclear weapons into Cuba.

When President Kennedy informed the nation on October 22, 1962, that Soviet nuclear weapon silos were being established on Cuba, the response from both the Soviet Union and from Cuba was one of denial. Soviet premier

Fidel Castro, address to the Cuban people, Havana, Cuba, October 23, 1962.

Nikita Khrushchev denied that the missiles existed, while Cuban dictator Fidel Castro stated that any weapons existing on Cuba were for defensive purposes only and had been imported to protect the Cuban people from any further aggression by the United States. In the following excerpt from a television and radio broadcast of October 23, 1962, to the people of Cuba, Castro argues that the accusations against Cuba by the Kennedy administration are another justification to proceed with military intervention operations in Cuba. Furthermore, he contends that attempts to invade Cuba are part of an already existing U.S. strategy to halt productive political and social advancements in the Western Hemisphere.

Announcer: Good evening, televiewers. All Cuba's radio and television stations are in network this evening to carry the statements by the Prime Minister of the revolutionary government and the secretary general of ORI [Organizaciones Revolucianarias Integrariias (Integrated Revolutionary Organizations)], Maj. Fidel Castro Ruz, at a particularly delicate time in the history of the world.

As you know, the United States has established a naval blockade of the Cuba archipelago, using as a pretext the arms acquired by Cuba for the exclusive purpose of assuring its defense against the U.S. aggressions.

Cuba has replied to this aggressive action by issuing the order of battle alert which places our people in arms on a war footing in a few hours.

Today the USSR [United Soviet Socialists Republic] replied to Kennedy's speech [of October 22, 1962] with a measured and firm statement firmly rejecting the assertions of the President of the United States and denouncing the danger of war created by U.S. aggression.

Today in Washington and New York the Council of the OAS [Organization of America States] was convoked by the United States, and the U.N. Security Council upon the request of Cuba, the Soviet Union, and the United States. Dr. Castro, what can you tell the people of Cuba concerning this new U.S. aggression?

The United States Attempts to Intervene in Cuba

Castro: Well, actually all these events are the culmination of a policy pursued by the United States, not (only by) the United States—the imperialists, the warmongers, and the most reactionary circles of the United States—against our country ever since the victory of the [Cuban] revolution [January 2, 1959]. All these measures do not surprise us. Measures of this type and others which we have had to endure are things which were logically to be expected from a type of government which is as reactionary and as lacking in respect of other peoples and other nations as is the U.S. Government.

However, the entire nation is familiar with all this history. Ever since the first day, since the very day of victory, which was a victory which cost our people so much sacrifice, they were able to see what the policy of U.S. Government would be toward us. This apart from the fact that our people, or part of our people—that part with the greatest amount of political awareness—was familiar with the history of the relations between the United States and Cuba ever since the end of the last century.

Actually all our progress, our independence, and our sovereignty have always been obscured by the policy of the Yankee governments. This intervention was an intervention for imperialist purposes—the Platt Amendment [giving the United States the right to establish a military base in Cuba and allowing the United States to intervene in Cuban affairs], the successive interventions, the seizure of the wealth of our country, the support given to the most reactionary and the most thieving governments. And finally, the support given to [ousted Cuban dictator Fulgencio] Batista, for we cannot forget and shall never forget that all the bombs they dropped upon us, and upon the people in the Sierra Maestra, were U.S.-made bombs. So, our people are acquainted with the entire procedure up to now.

U.S. Antagonism Is a Fruitless Effort

And how does the situation stand at present? The present situation is that this entire process of fighting was a useless battle by an empire waged against a small country; the useless, sterile,

Castro and Khrushchev contended that the U.S. government's accusations were used to justify a military invasion in Cuba.

and frustrated battle by an empire against a revolutionary government and against a revolution in a small country—underdeveloped and exploited until so recently.

Actually, why did the situation become acute? Why did it become critical? Simply because the United States failed in every design hitherto made against us. In short, it was defeated! The situation has grown worse from one defeat to the other. They had to choose between two things: To leave the Cuban revolution in peace or else to continue their policy of aggression until they endured the consequences which could be very bad for it.

So far they have been bad; they have been quite bad for U.S. prestige—I believe it has lost a considerable amount of prestige in this sterile battle against us. However, as unfavorable as this battle may have been, it could have been even more unfavorable. All its designs failed. The U.S. Government was accustomed to solving the problems of Latin America in a very simple way: first of all by a coup d'etat; and also through reactionary military cliques controlled by the embassies.

Whenever they could not solve problems by simple orders through their ambassadors, then it would be by means of revolutions, promoted rebellions, interventions, and all these things—interventions in our continent with which you are also acquainted. . . .

Communism in Cuba Halts U.S. Exploitation of Latin America

It is somewhat—I cannot call it amusing, because it is so ridiculous—it gives an impression of the mental poverty of the U.S. leaders such as, for example, a statement by [U.S. ambassador Adlai] Stevenson at the Security Council today to the effect that what Cuba could not be forgiven for was not its communism, or its socialism, or its revolution, but rather the fact that it introduced this problem into Latin America just at a time when the most extraordinary effort was being made for progress in Latin America. This was in reference to the Alliance. It is as though no one knew that the Alliance for Progress [Kennedy's plan for democratic and economic development in Latin America]—that facade, that false policy—is neither progress, nor alliance, nor anything but just another mockery.

But after all the agreements they reached, all the steps they took, and even all the credits they have given—and there were few, but those they did give—all this took place after the Cuban revolution. Thus we can say that without the Cuban revolution the imperialists would not have made the slightest effort to conceal their policy of exploitation, because the Alliance for Progress is nothing more than a formula to conceal their system of exploitation in Latin America. . . .

The United States Applies Economic Pressure

Along with this policy there came more economic aggressions: complete blockade—useless. By blockade I mean a complete ban on purchases of Cuban products and sales of products to

Cuba despite the fact that all our factories and transportation needed spare parts made in the United States.

That was not enough. All that was useless. They then began an even more aggressive policy. It was no longer a matter of banning the sales of our products in the United States, but of pursuing our products over the world—and, at the same time, of attempting to prevent all capitalist countries from selling to us. . . .

To sum it up, it has been the story of an uninterrupted chain of failures leading the imperialists, who have not resigned themselves, who will not resign themselves, despite the fact that they have no choice but to resign themselves—a series of more adventurous, more aggressive, and more dangerous steps for the sole purpose of destroying the Cuban revolution.

Another Act of Aggression

In the four years of the Cuban revolution's vigorous and healthy life they have not been able to make a dent in it. If we analyze the picture of our country and of our people we will see that the revolution is stronger than ever at this time. Thus, the failure of the attempt to destroy the Cuban revolution is what led to this latest step.

What is the latest step? It is the most temerarious and most dangerous adventure to world peace which has happened since the last world war.

The people were informed of the declaration of Mr. Kennedy made yesterday. During the day we had been receiving a series of reports about peculiar meetings, about peculiar things which were going on in Washington in connection with meetings with an officer from the Pentagon, meetings with political leaders of both parties, and meetings of the Security Council, plane movements, ship movements. And from all these reports we realized that it had something to do with us. We knew because of everything they had been doing before, of the policy pursued since the revolution, the warmongering campaign, hysteria, the joint resolution, and all those things.

We became aware that something could happen from one moment to another. However, inasmuch as they will not take us by surprise—because they have not taken us by surprise up to now and they will not take us by surprise—when Playa Giron occurred, they did not take us by surprise. When we became aware that something was happening and that some sort of action was imminent, we did not know exactly what it would be or from where it would come. Discussing the situation, the comrades decided that it was necessary to get our forces on the alert.

Cuban Forces Ready for Combat

That is why yesterday afternoon, at 5:40 P.M., the order for sounding the alarm for battle was given. The combat alarm is the highest degree of alert for the armed forces. We wanted to avoid having to take this measure unless it was in the face of something, of a very evident danger, because naturally all of our efforts, the efforts of our country, have for many months been devoted almost exclusively to increasing production and improving the economy. In reality, our country had, and has progressed very much in that field.

Naturally, every time a move of this nature is made, it implies making sacrifices in the field of production, no matter how much one tried to reconcile one thing with the other. And even though we have much more organization and experience, it is affected anyway. In the face of this situation, an order was decreed, and naturally all instructions in the case of a combat alarm were fulfilled in preparation for an aggression and against a danger of a surprise attack. At this moment, therefore, they cannot stage a surprise attack.

As you can see, gentlemen, we must be distrustful always. The same could have occurred—the type of movement that they were carrying out, which was the alleged maneuver in Vieques Island, a landing maneuver in Puerto Rico, to be aimed at Cuba, as in effect was done. They suspended the maneuvers, and we were alert, because one of their methods is to simulate a maneuver and launch an attack, to try to get by surprise the objectives they propose to reach.

The maneuvers were in progress, and in anticipation of something that might happen, such as a sudden attack by surprise, that order was given. Naturally, the declaration appeared in print later, but this declaration was nothing more than a confirmation of the Kennedy declaration; it just confirmed and justified the measures we had taken. Why was this? Simply because an imperialist adventure of this type implies such dangers that it is necessary to be in a complete state of alert.

After trying to justify it in a preamble in which the reasons he invoked are all reasons that have absolutely no foundation, he says that the armaments received by Cuba constitute a threat to the peace and the security of all of the Americas in a flagrant and reproachful defiance of the 1947 Rio de Janeiro Pact [a mutual defense treaty between the United States and Latin America]—an act that might have validity for those who continue in the fold of imperialism, but not or us.

U.S. Demands Mean Very Little to Castro

What are the traditions of this nation and the hemisphere? What are the traditions of this nation? What are the traditions of imperialist exploitation? The piratical sacking of our wealth and the exploitation of our workers? The tradition of submission and exploitation? Then, according to him, we violate the traditions of this continent, the joint resolution of the 87th Congress. What do we care about all of the resolutions? It is all the same to us, the 87th or the 7th or the 587th American Congress.

He speaks of the U.N. Charter. Precisely at the moment they are about to violate the U.N. Charter, they invoke the U.N. Charter against us. We have not violated in the least any of the U.N. Charter articles—not in the least. There is nothing that can be charged against us, nor can anyone say that we have violated any of its articles.

At the moment when they get ready to commit a flagrant and barefaced violation, they invoke the U.N. Charter. He says: "My own public warnings to the Soviet on 4 and 13 September" —what do we care about Mr. Kennedy's own personal warnings? They can matter only to him and his own people, but they do not concern us in the least.

Photographic Evidence of Missiles in Cuba

Adlai Stevenson

On October 23, 1962, U.S. ambassador to the United Nations, Adlai Stevenson, debated with Soviet Ambassador Valerian Zorin regarding the existence of nuclear weapons in Cuba. At this time, Ambassador Zorin denied the existence of nuclear weapons in Cuba and accused the United States of escalating Cold War tensions by establishing a naval blockade around Cuba. Zorin also declared that any attempts to prevent Soviet transports ships from reaching Cuba would be viewed as an act of aggression and could lead to war. The results of the debate were released in the *New York Times* and other major media publications worldwide. The impact of the debate only increased fear and tension. To the global community, it seemed clear that the United States and the Soviet Union were on the brink of a nuclear confrontation.

Two days later, on October 25, Ambassador Stevenson returned to the United Nations and confronted Ambassador Zorin a second time with evidence that nuclear silos existed in Cuba. U-2 spy planes had photographed the progress of the missile silo construction. Ambassador Stevenson presented the photographic evidence to the UN Security Council and to Ambassador Zorin. Zorin denied that these photographs represented nuclear missile silos. Several members of Kennedy's administration had little

Adlai Stevenson, testimony before the United Nations Security Council, October 25, 1962.

faith in Stevenson's ability to persuade the Security Council to act on behalf of the United States. They viewed the ambassador as a political relic who had served beyond his years of usefulness. The successful delivery of this speech, however, became the defining moment of Adlai Stevenson's political career as his presentation of evidence helped shore up the necessary global support behind the U.S. accusations against the Soviet Union.

I want to say to you, Mr. Zorin, that I do not have your talent for obfuscation, for distortion, for confusing language, and for doubletalk. And I must confess to you that I am glad that I do not!

But if I understood what you said, you said that my position had changed, that today I was defensive because we did not have the evidence to prove our assertions, that your Government had installed long-range missiles in Cuba.

Well, let me say something to you, Mr. Ambassador—we do have the evidence. We have it, and it is clear and it is incontrovertible. And let me say something else—those weapons must be taken out of Cuba.

Next, let me say to you that, if I understood you, with a trespass on credibility that excels your best, you said that our position had changed since I spoke here the other day [October 23, 1962] because of the pressures of world opinion and the majority of the United Nations. Well, let me say to you, sir, you are wrong again. We have had no pressure from anyone whatsoever. We came in here today to indicate our willingness to discuss [secretary general of the United Nations] Mr. U Thant's proposals, and that is the only change that has taken place.

Setting the Stage for Presenting Evidence

But let me also say to you sir, that there has been a change. You—the Soviet Union has sent these weapons to Cuba. You—the Soviet Union has upset the balance of power in the world. You—the Soviet Union has created this new danger, not the United States.

And you ask with a fine show of indignation why the President [John F. Kennedy] did not tell [Soviet ambassador to the United States] Mr. [Andrei] Gromyko on last Thursday about our evidence, at the very time that Mr. Gromyko was blandly denying to the President that the U.S.S.R. was placing such weapons on sites in the new world.

Well, I will tell you why—because we were assembling the evidence, and perhaps it would be instructive to the world to see how a Soviet official—how far he would go in perfidy. Perhaps we wanted to know if this country faced another example of nuclear deceit like that one a year ago, when in stealth, the Soviet Union broke the nuclear test moratorium.

And while we are asking questions, let me ask you why your Government—your Foreign Minister—deliberately, cynically deceived us about the nuclear build-up in Cuba.

And, finally, the other day, Mr. Zorin, I remind you that you did not deny the existence of these weapons. Instead, we heard that they had suddenly become defensive weapons. But today again if I heard you correctly, you now say that they do not exist, or that we haven't proved they exist, with another fine flood of rhetorical scorn.

All right, sir, let me ask you one simple question: Do you, Ambassador Zorin, deny that the U.S.S.R. has placed and is placing medium- and intermediate-range missiles and sites in Cuba? Yes or no—don't wait for the translation—yes or no?

(The Soviet representative refused to answer.)

You can answer yes or no. You have denied they exist. I want to know if I understood you correctly. I am prepared to wait for my answer until hell freezes over, if that's your decision. And I am also prepared to present the evidence in this room.

(The President called on the representative of Chile to speak, but Ambassador Stevenson continued as follows.)

I have not finished my statement. I asked you a question. I have had no reply to the question, and I will now proceed, if I may, to finish my statement.

I doubt if anyone in this room, except possibly the representative of the Soviet Union, has any doubt about the facts.

But in view of his statements and the statements of the Soviet Government up until last Thursday, when Mr. Gromyko denied the existence or any intention of installing such weapons in Cuba, I am going to make a portion of the evidence available right now. If you will indulge me for a moment, we will set up an easel here in the back of the room where I hope it will be visible to everyone.

Photographic Evidence Proves the Missiles Exist

The first of these exhibits shows an area north of the village of Candelaria, near San Cristóbal, southwest of Habana. A map, together with a small photograph, shows precisely where the area is in Cuba.

Stevenson presented evidence of nuclear missile silos in Cuba in order to gain UN support against the Soviet Union.

The first photograph shows the area in late August 1962; it was then, if you can see from where you are sitting, only a peaceful countryside.

The second photograph shows the same area one day last week. A few tents and vehicles had come into the area, new spur roads had appeared, and the main road had been improved.

The third photograph, taken only twenty-four hours later, shows facilities for a medium-range missile battalion installed. There are tents for 400 or 500 men. At the end of the new spur road there are seven 1,000-mile missile trailers. There are four launcher-erector mechanisms for placing these missiles in erect firing position. This missile is a mobile weapon, which can be moved rapidly from one place to another. It is identical with the 1,000-mile missiles which have been displayed in Moscow parades. All of this, I remind you, took place in twenty-four hours.

The second exhibit, which you can all examine at your leisure, shows three successive photographic enlargements of another missile base of the same type in the area of San Cristóbal. These enlarged photographs clearly show six of these missiles on trailers and three erectors.

And that is only one example of the first type of ballistic missile installation in Cuba.

A second type of installation is designed for a missile of intermediate range—a range of about 2,200 miles. Each site of this type has four launching pads.

The exhibit on this type of missile shows a launching area being constructed near Guanajay, southwest of the city of Habana. As in the first exhibit, a map and small photograph show this area as it appeared in late August 1962, when no military activities were apparent.

A second large photograph shows the same area about six weeks later. Here you will see a very heavy construction effort, to push the launching area to rapid completion. The pictures show two large concrete bunkers or control centers in process of construction, one between each pair of launching pads. They show heavy concrete retaining walls being erected to shelter vehicles and equipment from rocket blast-off. They show cable scars leading from the launch pads to the bunkers. They show a large reinforced concrete building under construction. A building with a heavy arch may well be intended as the storage area for the nuclear warheads. The installation is not yet complete, and no warheads are yet visible.

The next photograph shows a closer view of the same intermediate-range launch site. You can clearly see one of the pairs of large concrete launch pads, with a concrete building from which launching operations for three pads are controlled. Other details are visible, such as fuel tanks.

And that is only one example, one illustration, of the work being furnished in Cuba on intermediate-range missile bases.

Photographs Reveal Bombers and Deployment Facilities

Now, in addition to missiles, the Soviet Union is installing other offensive weapons in Cuba. The next photograph is of an airfield at San Julián in western Cuba. On this field you will see twenty-two crates designed to transport the fuselages of Soviet llyushin-28 bombers. Four of the aircraft are uncrated, and one is partially assembled. These bombers, sometimes known as Beagles, have an operating radius of about 750 miles and are capable of carrying nuclear weapons. At the same field you can see one of the surface-to-air antiaircraft guided missile bases, with six missiles per base, which now ring the entire coastline of Cuba.

Another set of two photographs covers still another area of deployment of medium-range missiles in Cuba. These photographs are on a larger scale than the others and reveal many details of an improved field-type launch site. One photograph provides an overall view of most of the site; you can see clearly three of the four launching pads. The second photograph displays details of two of these pads. Even an eye untrained in photographic interpretation can clearly see the buildings in which the missiles are checked out and maintained ready to fire, a missile trailer, trucks to move missiles out to the launching pad, erectors to raise the missiles to launching position, tank trucks to provide fuel, vans from which the missile firing is controlled, in short, all of the requirements to maintain, load, and fire these terrible weapons.

These weapons, gentlemen, these launching pads, these planes—of which we have illustrated only a fragment—are a part of a much larger weapons complex, what is called a weapons system.

To support this build-up, to operate these advanced weapons systems, the Soviet Union has sent a large number of military personnel to Cuba—a force now mounting to several thousand men.

These photographs, as I say, are available to members for detailed examination in the Trusteeship Council room following this meeting. There I will have one of my aides who will gladly explain them to you in such detail as you may require.

I have nothing further to say at this time.

(After another statement by the Soviet representative, Ambassador Stevenson replied as follows:)

Soviet Ambassador Still Denies Missiles Exist

Mr. President and gentlemen, I won't detain you but one minute.

I have not had a direct answer to my question. The representative of the Soviet Union says that the official answer of the U.S.S.R. was the Tass [Soviet news agency] statement that they don't need to locate missiles in Cuba. Well, I agree—they don't need to. But the question is, have they missiles in Cuba—and that question remains unanswered. I knew it would be.

As to the authenticity of the photographs, which Mr. Zorin has spoken about with such scorn, I wonder if the Soviet Union would ask its Cuban colleague to permit a U.N. team to go to these sites. If so, I can assure you that we can direct them to the proper places very quickly.

And now I hope that we can get down to business, that we can stop this sparring. We know the facts, and so do you, sir, and we are ready to talk about them. Our job here is not to score debating points. Our job, Mr. Zorin, is to save the peace. And if you are ready to try, we are.

Chapter 2

Thirteen Days in October: The Crisis Unfolds

U.S. Policy on the Eve of the Crisis

Bertram B. Johansson

When Fidel Castro led the Cuban revolution and overthrew President Fulgencio Batista in 1958, many nations, including the United States, did not expect Castro to embrace communism. Castro's decision to install a Communist government was seen as a threat to the peace and security of the Western Hemisphere, and the United States took immediate steps to counteract this new Communist presence. The United States responded initially with political and economic pressure by placing trade embargoes on Cuban imports. In 1961 the Kennedy administration sought a military solution, secretly backing the training of Cuban exiles as mercenaries who would attempt to oust Castro from power. The resulting Bay of Pigs invasion failed. In the aftermath of this failed attack, Castro sought support from the Soviet Union. The Soviets recognized the potential advantage Cuba provided. Over the next year they began exporting weapons and personnel to Cuba to increase their own presence in the Western Hemisphere.

In the following *Christian Science Monitor* article from October 20, 1962, two full days before President Kennedy's announcement of a nuclear crisis, Latin American editor Bertram B. Johansson explores the impact of the current U.S. policy toward Cuba. He outlines the series of political pressures placed on Cuba by the United States in retaliation for its importation of non-nuclear Russian weaponry and personnel. Johansson also contends that such political

Bertram B. Johansson, "Cuba and the American Conscience," *The Christian Science Monitor*, vol. 54, October 20, 1962, p. 18.

pressure may hasten the collapse of the Cuban Communist regime and create an increased toll on American resources due to an influx of Cuban refugees seeking aid from the United States.

Cuba has popped up like a cork from the depths of the American conscience as the most emotionally charged issue in the election campaign [congressional and gubernatorial races] which still has two more weeks to run.

While President Kennedy steadily maintains that the domestic economy is the pertinent issue of the midterm elections, Republican top command strategists label Cuba as the "dominant" issue, and a "symbol of the tragic irresolution of the [Kennedy] administration."

Democrats remind their critics that "Fidel Castro took power in Cuba in 1958—during the Republican administration."

Antiphonally, President Kennedy charges Republicans (in this case he meant Sen. Homer E. Capehart of Indian) had indulged in "rash and irresponsible talk" suggesting possible invasion of Cuba.

The President speaks sharply of "those self-appointed generals and admirals who want to send someone else's son to war and who consistently voted against the instruments of peace."

In Washington, high sources outlined Cuban policy this past week as: no invasion, squeezing the Cuban economy, forcing the Soviet Union to pay dearly for keeping the Cuban economy viable, stopping hemisphere Communist subversion, and "waiting" for the breaks.

United States Concerned but Not Panicked

Former President [Dwight D.] Eisenhower, responding to charges of foreign policy "drift" during his administration, threatened to break his silence on foreign policy questions, adding he saw little constructive in Mr. Kennedy's 21 months of foreign affairs management.

The Soviet Union through its news agencies said the people of the United States have become "hysterical" over the Cuban question.

By contrast, *Newsweek* magazine, in a nationwide survey of the Cuban question, found that "nearly all Americans are deeply concerned—but not panicked—by the presence of Soviet arms and 'technicians' 90 miles from the Florida keys," and that "about 90 per cent don't want to invade Cuba now."

Journalists Present a Light Mood While Military Prepares

Art Buchwald, irrepressible humorist of the *New York Herald Tribune*, balanced some of the concern about Cuba as he wrote in his copyrighted syndicated column:

"The Americans are very upset because Russia has been supplying Cuba with arms and technicians and therefore it's become a Communist threat in the hemisphere. But the issue has become clouded because former Vice-President [Richard] Nixon, who is running for Governor of California, says there is a Communist threat in California, which his opponent, Gov. [Pat] Brown, has done nothing about. Now California is less than 90 miles away from the United States, and therefore some hotheads want to blockade California instead of Cuba."

In the meantime, the United States went ahead with its more mundane, humorless preparations to safeguard its flanks. As quietly as it could, the Pentagon, moving to counter a build-up of jet MIGs in Cuba, shifted a squadron to 1,400-miles-an-hour Navy Phantom jet fighters to southern Florida.

The move came three days after Undersecretary of State George W. Ball told a congressional committee Cuba soon will probably have 25 to 30 of the most modern Soviet-built jet fighters which normally carry air-to-air missiles, plus 60 older MIGs. A Pentagon spokesman said the move was related to Mr. Ball's testimony.

The F4B Phantom is rated as the Navy's fastest, highest flying, and longest range fighter with the greatest firepower of any Navy fighter plane. It mounts both Sparrow and Sidewinder missiles and with detection and tracking systems that make it capable of destroying faster-than-sound as well as slower planes by day or night, in all weather.

United States Prepares to Ban Soviet-Bloc Goods

In another sector of applying pressure on Cuba, the United States went about preparing to issue a ban in all United States ports on ships carrying Soviet-bloc goods to Cuba.

The proposal is not meeting with enthusiastic approval from all the nation's allies. The British Ambassador to the United States says his government is powerless to halt British trade with Cuba.

"We have no laws to interfere with shipping," said Sir David Ormsby Gore in a Philadelphia news conference. He said the British Government halted arms shipments to Cuba two years ago and the volume of its trade was dropped from $42,000,000 three years ago to an expected $8,400,000 this year.

He rendered the observation that "there is evidence from history that a blockade does not bring down a dictator. Instead, it sometimes creates sympathy for the tyrant, who can use it for propaganda purposes."

This poses neatly one of the dilemmas facing the Kennedy administration, especially before the elections. There is the demand from the American public to "do something" about Cuba.

The Problem of Cuban Refugees

But if a Castro Marxist-Leninist regime should fall while United States economic pressures are being exerted on Cuba, then, some reason, it would not have been demonstrated that a Communist-supported regime had fallen of its own weight and confusion.

On the other hand, if the United States stands idly by and allows a Communist government to succeed in Cuba and to exhibit a prosperous though subsidized economy this course would appear unpolitic in the current United States context.

The Cuban refugee problem, already expressed in terms of crowded living quarters in Miami and several other cities, separated families, unemployment or menial employment when it is available, and the necessity for the United States to supply relief funds for needy Cubans, was erupting in other forms, as well.

Uppermost in the thought of most of the estimated 200,000 Cuban exiles now in the United States is the desire for Cuban freedom, and their return to a free Cuba. This desire has taken from in raids on Cuban ports by small exile organizations, the raids appearing sometimes to come from United States territory.

This is extremely embarrassing, at times, to the State Department, which is keen just now on not being pushed into compromising positions on Berlin or other world hot spots.

The remembrance is still vivid in Washington of how quickly the Soviet Union marched into Hungary at the time of the Suez crisis[1] when the British offered resistance in Egypt.

Republican pressures on the Cuban issues have been so telling in the Democratic camp that Vice-President Lyndon B. Johnson has had to enunciate definitely for the administration that current United States policy is to get rid of the Soviet Castro regime in Cuba. That was two weeks ago, during a campaign speech in Texas. The next week he followed up with a statement that Cuba is being contained and isolated.

1. In 1956 Britain and France invaded Egypt to gain control of the Suez Canal. The Soviet Union used the invasion as an excuse to annex Hungary.

The U.S. Quarantine of Cuba Raises the Stakes

Robert R. Brunn

On October 24, 1962, the U.S. Navy intercepted the first Soviet tanker attempting to pass though the naval quarantine. The navy determined that the ship was not carrying any military cargo and allowed the tanker to continue on to Cuba. Although this particular ship was not boarded by U.S. personnel, a dozen other Soviet tankers that had been close behind this one turned around, choosing not to challenge the U.S. quarantine. In this October 25, 1962, article from the *Christian Science Monitor*, journalist Robert R. Brunn examines the incident and explores its possible ramifications for U.S.-Soviet relations during this time of crisis. Brunn also states that the United Nations, in an attempt to prevent any further escalation of the crisis, suggests that the United States use the successful quarantine attempt to foster continued peace talks between the two superpowers and requests that the United States accept a moratorium on further quarantine activities until a peaceful solution to the crisis is implemented.

The stealthy, knifelike pre–Pearl Harbor–type tactic of the Soviet thrust in Cuba is being blocked so far by an unyielding limited United States action.

In a somber Washington the United States moves with extreme caution.

Robert R. Brunn, "Cuba Quarantine Holds: U.S. Blunts Soviet Thrust," *The Christian Science Monitor*, October 25, 1962, p. 1.

The first Cuban-bound ship intercepted by the United States Navy was a Russian tanker and it was allowed to continue without being boarded after it was determined it carried no offensive arms, the Pentagon reported. A dozen other Soviet ships were said to have turned back for fear of running into the American ban on shipment of offensive arms to Cuba.

Having chosen its own time and place in which to check Soviet aggression, the United States may well have upset a Communist timetable tied to Berlin [refers to current negotiations over potential Soviet takeover of West Berlin].

Repercussions of the Naval Blockade

Now, informed sources believe [Soviet] Premier Nikita S. Khrushchev is trying to fog up the atmosphere with a screen of words, and interesting talk about a summit talk while, it is speculated, he and the Presidium [governing body of the Soviet Union] ponder further steps.

What follows is a summation from informed sources of the principal factors and possible repercussions flowing out from the United States decision to react massively to the Soviet power drive:

• United Nations moratorium. Secretary-General U Thant's proposal for a two- or three-week moratorium with a suspension of the quarantine is considered unacceptable by the United States in its present form.

No guarantee against further delivery of arms to Cuba is provided in the plan to stop the Soviet military build-up. On-the-spot UN inspection would be necessary to be sure the missile sites are being dismantled or, at a minimum, work is stopped.

• Summit talks. To move rapidly on the apparent Khrushchev proposal for talks made in a telegram to Bertrand Russell[1] would be unwise.

First the question of the approaching ships must be eliminated.

1. British philosopher who was a proponent for nuclear disarmament

Soviets Pledge for Peace Not War

Next, the United States is not exactly in a mood for a Khrushchev-Kennedy meeting with 1,000- and 2,500-mile range missiles pointed at the United States, possibly with nuclear warheads available.

The Soviet words are taking the familiar Soviet "peace pose." Premier Khrushchev spoke of a summit talk when the United States landed troops in Lebanon in 1958 [to help prevent a hostile takeover by the Soviet Union] but it never took place.

Mr. Khrushchev said "take no rash decisions. . . . Avert a war"—the Soviet Union will "not let itself be provoked." This message may have taken some of the edge off the tension but it has not changed the basic problem of missiles in Cuba.

A Khrushchev note to President Kennedy handed to [U.S.] Ambassador [to the Soviet Union] Foy Kohler, it is understood, did not contain any direct proposal for a summit meeting.

• Soviet tactics. Apart from the Communist-bloc ships approach, any action by the Soviets is the form of a riposte to counter the quarantine effect may come slowly.

The United States Stands Firm

Premier Khrushchev is capable of a good deal of caution if brought up short. But to protect his political position is a tough response inescapable?

A Soviet response around its power periphery is considered likely, but the timing of any move is, of course, uncertain. Berlin still is given priority as a major possibility.

Washington knows that the Soviet Union completely understands there is little "give" in the Western response plan.

A View of the Blockade from the Air

J. Frank Diggs

The naval quarantine of Cuba officially began on October 24, 1962, and covered roughly six shipping channels between the tiny islands around Cuba and Puerto Rico. In this eyewitness account of the quarantine from the cockpit of a U.S. Navy plane, *U.S. News & World Report* staff writer J. Frank Diggs comments on the scale of the operation. From his vantage point he observed that the navy ships formed two separate blockade screens. An initial line of U.S. destroyers covered each of the shipping channels around Cuba. Behind them was a larger force of aircraft carriers and destroyers that formed a blockade screen in the event a Cuban-bound ship should break through the quarantine. Diggs reports that from the air it appears the United States is well equipped to conduct such a massive quarantine of Cuba.

The blockade, as it got under way in the Caribbean, was something to watch. At 10 A.M. on October 24 [1962], when the big "quarantine" of Cuba officially began, I was flying in a U.S. Navy plane over the blockade area. During the next four hours, we flew a course parallel to the north coast of Cuba—crossing all of the shipping lanes that Soviet vessels would have to use to reach Cuban ports.

The American blockade force was now spread out below, over thousands of square miles of blue Caribbean. From 10,000 feet in the air, the altitude maintained by our two-engine Navy transport, it was an impressive sight.

J. Frank Diggs, "How the Blockade Began," *U.S. News & World Report,* vol. LIII, November 5, 1962, p. 52.

As we flew west from Puerto Rico, the first vessels we spotted were three fast-moving U.S. warships, apparently headed for the much-traveled Windward Passage between Cuba and Haiti. One of the gray vessels looked like a cruiser, the others like destroyer escorts.

Then a group of four relatively slow freighters appeared. Their nationality was unknown. Although well within the blockade area, they were not headed for Cuba and were not stopped.

By now, we were over Grand Turk Island, where the big U.S. missile-tracking station was helping to keep tabs on Cuba-bound shipping.

Pointing at the big radar installations on Grand Turk, a naval officer on the plane commented: "With those radars, a mosquito couldn't get through without its position being marked up by somebody's grease pencil."

Viewing the Shipping Lanes by Plane

Flying a course that stayed roughly 150 miles from the Cuban coast, we soon could see how this blockade would be operated. We flew over a long series of islands that both screened Cuba from the open Atlantic and also channeled all ships from Europe through the passages between islands.

Russia's supply ships, in other words, had to pass through one of only half a dozen channels between the little tropical islands we were flying over—Caicos, Mayaguana, Long Island, Great Guana Cay, Andros.

We now began to spot U.S. destroyers below, all traveling at apparent high speed and operating singly, each evidently covering a channel between islands. There were no aircraft carriers this close in. These and other larger craft were reported forming a reserve force behind the blockade screen.

With clear weather and few clouds, you could see for great distances at this altitude. But there was little civilian shipping in sight, much less than I had seen over the same area just a few days before. There were a few sailboats, but no fishing boats or cruise ships, and as yet no Havana-bound freighters.

Finally, near Andros—the biggest of the Bahama Islands—we spotted what we had been especially watching for. This was a ship resembling an oil tanker with its superstructure in the rear. It could be the Soviet ship, equipped with an outsized hold, that was reported to be conveying big missiles from Russia to Havana.

This big ship was headed due west. It could be bound for the Florida Straits and New Orleans, or for the western tip of Cuba which includes Havana.

A closer look confirmed that it was merely a tanker. The blockade forces apparently had checked it out, as well. A destroyer, you could see, was not far away.

Just a few ships, thus, could effectively cover the approaches to Cuba, were on station, at work.

A Sizable Blockade

A far larger force—sea and air—had been assembled by this time, however. The nucleus of this blockade fleet was the force of 40 warships that had been scheduled to conduct maneuvers off Puerto Rico. Most of these sailed out secretly on October 21. By October 24 they had been joined by more warships from several East Coast ports. Norfolk, Va., and the big base at Mayport, Fla., near Jacksonville, contributed the biggest number.

Involved, by this time, were several carriers, some cruisers, dozens of destroyers, even some submarines.

Aircraft were involved as well, but not in great numbers. We saw none in a four-hour flight across the blockade area. The big function of the blockade planes, at this stage, was to spot by their high-altitude radar all ships coming into the Caribbean, then to make a quick check on each one to find its nationality, type and course. It was the warships that were actively carrying out the blockade—and prepared to use force if necessary. Nonetheless, hundreds of planes had been assembled.

You could see that the U.S. this time appeared to have more than enough strength on hand, in position to carry out an effective blockade.

A Secret Letter from Khrushchev to Kennedy

Nikita Khrushchev

On October 26, 1962, Soviet premier Nikita Khrushchev sent a secret telegram to President Kennedy in order to seek an agreement regarding the crisis. In the telegram, excerpted here, Khrushchev expresses concern at the pace of the crisis. He appeals to Kennedy's sense of reason, knowing that neither he nor Kennedy seeks a nuclear confrontation. He tries to explain away the presence of nuclear missiles in Cuba as defensive in nature, but in the end he admits that the United States understandably would view the weapons as offensive. Khrushchev expresses a willingness to withdraw the missile bases from Cuba on the condition that the United States not conduct an invasion of the island.

Dear Mr. President:

I have received your letter of October 25. From your letter, I got the feeling that you have some understanding of the situation which has developed and (some) sense of responsibility. I value this.

Now we have already publicly exchanged our evaluations of the events around Cuba and each of us has set forth his explanation and his understanding of these events. Consequently, I would judge that, apparently, a continuation of an exchange of opinions at such a distance, even in the form of secret let-

Nikita Khrushchev, "Department of State Telegram Transmitting Letter from Chairman Khrushchev to President Kennedy, October 26, 1962," *Department of State Bulletin*, November 9, 1973, pp. 640–45.

ters, will hardly add anything to that which one side has already said to the other.

I think you will understand me correctly if you are really concerned about the welfare of the world. Everyone needs peace: both capitalists, if they have not lost their reason, and, still more, Communists, people who know how to value not only their own lives but, more than anything, the lives of the peoples. We, Communists, are against all wars between states in general and have been defending the cause of peace since we came into the world. We have always regarded war as a calamity, and not as a game nor as a means for the attainment of definite goals, nor, all the more, as a goal in itself. Our goals are clear, and the means to attain them is labor. War is our enemy and a calamity for all the peoples.

It is thus that we, Soviet people, and, together with US, other peoples as well, understand the questions of war and peace. I can, in any case, firmly say this for the peoples of the Socialist countries, as well as for all progressive people who want peace, happiness, and friendship among peoples.

A War Between Superpowers Is Senseless

I see, Mr. President, that you too are not devoid of a sense of anxiety for the fate of the world and an understanding of what war entails. What would a war give you? You are threatening us with war. But you well know that the very least which you would receive in reply would be that you would experience the same consequences as those which you sent us. And that must be clear to us, people invested with authority, trust, and responsibility. We must not succumb to intoxication and petty passions, regardless of whether elections are impending in this or that country, or not impending. These are all transient things, but if indeed war should break out, then it would not be in our power to stop it, for such is the logic of war. I have participated in two wars and know that war ends when it has rolled through cities and villages, everywhere sowing death and destruction.

In the name of the Soviet Government and the Soviet people, I assure you that your conclusions regarding offensive weapons on Cuba are groundless. It is apparent from what you have written me that our conceptions are different on this score, or rather, we have different estimates of these or those military means. Indeed, in reality, the same forms of weapons can have different interpretations.

The Difference Between Offensive and Defensive Weapons

You are a military man and, I hope, will understand me. Let us take for example a simple cannon. What sort of means is this: offensive or defensive? A cannon is a defensive means if it is set up to defend boundaries or a fortified area. But if one concentrates artillery, and adds to it the necessary number of troops, then the same cannons do become an offensive means, because they prepare and clear the way for infantry to attack. The same happens with missile-nuclear weapons as well, with any type of this weapon.

You are mistaken if you think that any of our means on Cuba are offensive. However, let us not quarrel now. It is apparent that I will not be able to convince you of this. But I say to you: You, Mr. President, are a military man and should understand: Can one attack, if one has on one's territory even an enormous quantity of missiles of various effective radiuses and various power, but using only these means. These missiles are a means of extermination and destruction. But one cannot attack with these missiles, even nuclear missiles of a power of 100 megatons because only people, troops, can attack. Without people, any means however powerful cannot be offensive.

How can one, consequently, give such a completely incorrect interpretation as you are now giving, to the effect that some sort of means on Cuba are offensive. All the means located there, and I assure you of this, have a defensive character, are on Cuba solely for the purposes of defense, and we have sent them to Cuba at the request of the Cuban Government. You, however, say that these are offensive means.

Attacking the United States Is Suicide

But, Mr. President, do you really seriously think that Cuba can attack the United States and that even we together with Cuba can attack you from the territory of Cuba? Can you really think that way? How is it possible? We do not understand this. Has something so new appeared in military strategy that one can think that it is possible to attack thus. I say precisely attack, and not destroy, since barbarians, people who have lost their sense, destroy.

I believe that you have no basis to think this way. You can regard us with distrust, but, in any case, you can be calm in this regard, that we are of sound mind and understand perfectly well that if we attack you, you will respond the same way. But you too will receive the same that you hurl against us. And I think that you also understand this. My conversation with you in Vienna[1] gives me the right to talk to you this way.

This indicates that we are normal people, that we correctly understand and correctly evaluate the situation. Consequently, how can we permit the incorrect actions which you ascribe to us? Only lunatics or suicides, who themselves want to perish and to destroy the whole world before they die, could do this. We, however, want to live and do not at all want to destroy your country. We want something quite different: To compete with your country on a peaceful basis. We quarrel with you, we have differences on ideological questions. But our view of the world consists in this, that ideological questions, as well as economic problems, should be solved not by military means, they must be solved on the basis of peaceful competition, i.e. as this is understood in capitalist society, on the basis of competition. We have proceeded and are proceeding from the fact that the peaceful co-existence of the two different social-political systems, now existing in the world, is necessary, that it is necessary to assure a stable peace. That is the sort of principle we hold.

The Naval Blockade Is Unfounded Aggression Toward Russia

You have now proclaimed piratical measures, which were employed in the Middle Ages, when ships proceeding in international waters were attacked, and you have called this "a

1. In June 1961, Kennedy met with Khrushchev in Vienna to discuss a nuclear test ban treaty.

quarantine" around Cuba. Our vessels, apparently, will soon enter the zone which your Navy is patrolling. I assure you that these vessels, now bound for Cuba, are carrying the most innocent peaceful cargoes. Do you really think that we only occupy ourselves with the carriage of so-called offensive weapons, atomic and hydrogen bombs? Although perhaps your military people imagine that these (cargoes) are some sort of special type of weapon, I assure you that they are the most ordinary peaceful products.

Consequently, Mr. President, let us show good sense. I assure you that on those ships, which are bound for Cuba, there are no weapons at all. The weapons which were necessary for the defense of Cuba are already there. I do not want to say that there were not any shipments of weapons at all. No, there were such shipments. But now Cuba has already received the necessary means of defense.

I don't know whether you can understand me and believe me. But I should like to have you believe in yourself and to agree that one cannot give way to passions; it is necessary to control them. And in what direction are events now developing? If you stop the vessels, then, as you yourself know, that would be piracy. If we started to do that with regard to your ships, then you would also be as indignant as we and the whole world now are. One cannot give another interpretation to such actions, because one cannot legalize lawlessness. If this were permitted, then there would be no peace, there would also be no peaceful co-existence. We should then be forced to put into effect the necessary measures of a defensive character to protect our interests in accordance with international law. Why should this be done? To what would all this lead?

An Appeal to Diplomacy for World Peace

Let us normalize relations. We have received an appeal from the Acting Secretary General of the UN, U Thant, with his proposals. I have already answered him. His proposals come to this, that our side should not transport armaments of any kind to Cuba during a certain period of time, while negotiations are being conducted—and we are ready to enter such negotiations

—and the other side should not undertake any sort of piratical actions against vessels engaged in navigation on the high seas. I consider these proposals reasonable. This would be a way out of the situation which has been created, which would give the peoples the possibility of breathing calmly. You have asked what happened, what evoked the delivery of weapons to Cuba? You have spoken about this to our Minister of Foreign Affairs. I will tell you frankly, Mr. President, what evoked it.

We were very grieved by the fact—I spoke about it in Vienna —that a landing took place[2] that an attack on Cuba was committed, as a result of which many Cubans perished. You yourself told me then that this had been a mistake. I respected that explanation. You repeated it to me several times, pointing out that not everybody occupying a high position would acknowledge his mistakes as you had done. I value such frankness. For my part, I told you that we too possess no less courage; we also acknowledged those mistakes which had been committed during the history of our state, and not only acknowledged, but sharply condemned them.

If you are really concerned about the peace and welfare of your people, and this is your responsibility as President, then I, as the Chairman of the Council of Ministers, am concerned for my people. Moreover, the preservation of world peace should be our joint concern, since if, under contemporary conditions, war should break out, it would be a war not only between the reciprocal claims, but a world wide cruel and destructive war.

Assistance to Cuba Stems from Concern over Invasion

Why have we proceeded to assist Cuba with military and economic aid? The answer is: We have proceeded to do so only for reasons of humanitarianism. At one time, our people itself had a revolution, when Russia was still a backward country. We were attacked then. We were the target of attack by many countries. The USA participated in that adventure. This has

2. refers to the Bay of Pigs Invasion at Playa de Girón, April 1961

been recorded by participants in the aggression against our country. A whole book has been written about this by General [William] Graves, who, at that time, commanded the US Expeditionary Corps. Graves called it "The American Adventure in Siberia."

We know how difficult it is to accomplish a revolution and how difficult it is to reconstruct a country on new foundations. We sincerely sympathize with Cuba and the Cuban people, but we are not interfering in questions of domestic structure, we are not interfering in their affairs. The Soviet Union desires to help the Cubans build their life as they themselves wish and that others should not hinder them.

You once said that the United States was not preparing an invasion. But you also declared that you sympathized with the Cuban counter-revolutionary emigrants, that you support them and would help them to realize their plans against the present Government of Cuba. It is also not a secret to anyone that the threat of armed attack, aggression, has constantly hung, and continues to hang over Cuba. It was only this which impelled us to respond to the request of the Cuban Government to furnish it aid for the strengthening of the defensive capacity of this country.

If assurances were given by the President and the Government of the United States that the USA itself would not participate in an attack on Cuba and would restrain others from actions of this sort, if you would recall your fleet, this would immediately change everything. I am not speaking for Fidel Castro, but I think that he and the Government of Cuba, evidently, would declare demobilization and would appeal to the people to get down to peaceful labor. Then, too, the question of armaments would disappear, since, if there is no threat, then armaments are a burden for every people. Then too, the question of the destruction, not only of the armaments which you call offensive, but of all other armaments as well, would look different.

I spoke in the name of the Soviet Government in the United Nations and introduced a proposal for the disbandment of all armies and for the destruction of all armaments. How then can I now count on those armaments?

Khrushchev Offers a Solution

Armaments bring only disasters. When one accumulates them, this damages the economy, and if one puts them to use, then they destroy people on both sides. Consequently, only a madman can believe that armaments are the principal means in the life of society. No, they are an enforced loss of human energy, and what is more are for the destruction of man himself. If people do not show wisdom, then in the final analysis they will come to a clash, like blind moles, and then reciprocal extermination will begin.

Let us therefore show statesmanlike wisdom. I propose: We, for our part, will declare that our ships, bound for Cuba, will not carry any kind of armaments. You would declare that the United States will not invade Cuba with its forces and will not support any sort of forces which might intend to carry out an invasion of Cuba. Then the necessity for the presence of our military specialists in Cuba would disappear.

Mr. President, I appeal to you to weigh well what the aggressive, piratical actions, which you have declared the USA intends to carry out in international waters, would lead to. You yourself know that any sensible man simply cannot agree with this, cannot recognize your right to such actions.

If you did this as the first step towards the unleashing of war, well then, it is evident that nothing else is left to us but to accept this challenge of yours. If, however, you have not lost your self-control and sensibly conceive what this might lead to, then, Mr. President, we and you ought not now to pull on the ends of the rope in which you have tied the knot of war, because the more the two of us pull, the tighter that knot will be tied. And a moment may come when that knot will be tied so tight that even he who tied it will not have the strength to untie it, and then it will be necessary to cut that knot, and what that would mean is not for me to explain to you, because you yourself understand perfectly of what terrible forces our countries dispose.

Consequently, if there is no intention to tighten that knot and thereby to doom the world to the catastrophe of thermonuclear war, then let us not only relax the forces pulling on the ends of the rope, let us take measures to untie that knot. We are ready for this.

We welcome all forces which stand on positions of peace. Consequently, I expressed gratitude to Mr. Bertrand Russell[3] too, who manifests alarm and concern for the fate of the world, and I readily responded to the appeal of the Acting Secretary General of the UN, U Thant.

There, Mr. President, are my thoughts, which, if you agreed with them, could put an end to that tense situation which is disturbing all peoples.

These thoughts are dictated by a sincere desire to relieve the situation, to remove the threat of war.

Respectfully yours,
N. Khrushchev

3. a respected peace advocate who communicated with both Kennedy and Khrushchev during the crisis on the danger of nuclear war

Kennedy Offers Khrushchev a Deal

Robert T. Hartmann

President John F. Kennedy and Soviet premier Nikita Khrushchev both sought a peaceful resolution to the Cuban crisis. Both men recognized that any military confrontation involving the use of nuclear weapons would mean the certain destruction of both nations, but both leaders remained unwilling to back down without ensuring the receipt of certain concessions. On October 27, 1962, Khrushchev sent a communiqué to Kennedy stating that he wanted the United States to withdraw its nuclear missiles from the Turkish border, stop all surveillance flights over Cuba, and ensure that the U.S. military not invade Cuba. Although Khrushchev promised to remove the nuclear missiles from Cuba if the United States capitulated to these requests, Kennedy declared that until the continued construction of missile silos stopped and all nuclear missiles were removed from Cuba, no consideration would be given to Khrushchev's demands.

In this October 28, 1962, *Los Angeles Times* article, Robert T. Hartmann reports on the components of the current peace proposal. He focuses on Kennedy's willingness to consider Khrushchev's demands after the nuclear weapons are removed from Cuba and the missile silos are dismantled. Hartmann is an award-winning journalist, editor, and writer. He began working for the *Los Angeles Times* as a reporter after returning to the United States from World War II, and in 1948 he became that paper's youngest editorial writer.

United States Would Lift Blockade If Russians Remove Missiles from Cuba

President [John F.] Kennedy Saturday night told Premier [Nikita] Khrushchev he is willing to call off the U.S. quarantine of Cuba and open negotiations at the United Nations "this weekend" toward permanent solution of the Cuban problem if Russia will remove its missiles under U.N. [United Nations] supervision and send no more.

The President's reply to the most serious of two Khrushchev messages—one public for propaganda purposes and the other private and hitherto undisclosed—indicated that Mr. Kennedy considers the Soviet leader's confidential terms "generally acceptable as I understand them."

The White House reply was made public by Press Secretary [Pierre] Salinger late Saturday night after day-long tension had been compounded by reports of a missing U.S. reconnaissance plane in the Caribbean area and persistent Washington warnings that the Soviet 2,200 and 1,000-mile ballistic missile bases in Cuba were being rushed to completion.

Removal of Missiles from Turkey Not Mentioned

There was no mention in Mr. Kennedy's reply of the widely publicized Khrushchev proposal, broadcast by radio Moscow Saturday even before it was received at the White House, that the Soviets would dismantle their Cuban missiles in return for withdrawal of NATO IRBM [Intermediate Range Ballistic Missiles] installations in Turkey.

Some 30 Jupiter missiles have been stationed since 1958 in Turkey, the only NATO [North Atlantic Treaty Organization] ally bordering on the USSR [Union of Soviet Socialist Republics]. Earlier, the White House flatly rejected this trade.

The only concession the United States made was an offer to give the U.N. assurances against an American invasion of Cuba which had been considered imminent if work on the Soviet missile bases did not stop.

Kennedy and Khrushchev are pictured during 1961 talks in Vienna. Between October 26 and 28, 1962, they exchanged secret telegrams in an attempt to peacefully resolve the crisis.

The text of Khrushchev's private message was not released but the President in reply stated:

As I read your letter, the key elements of your proposal—which seem generally acceptable as I understand them—are as follows:

Components of the Proposal

"1—You would agree to remove these weapons systems from Cuba under appropriate United Nations' operation and supervision: and undertake with suitable safeguards, to halt the further introduction of such weapons systems into Cuba.

"2—We, on our part, would agree—upon the establishment of adequate arrangements through the United Nations to ensure the carrying out and continuation of these commitments —(a) to remove promptly the quarantine measures now in effect and (b) to give assurances against an invasion of Cuba. I am confident that other nations of the Western Hemisphere would be prepared to do likewise."

Khrushchev had already, in an exchange of messages with U.N. Acting Secretary General Thant as mediator, agreed not to try to run the U.S. blockade of Cuba, and Mr. Kennedy had tentatively consented to minimize contacts between American and Soviet ships for the next few days. But he emphasized that work on the Cuban missile sites must be suspended at once or this country would feel free to take necessary action in self-defense.

To underscore this point, Defense Secretary [Robert] McNamara, a few minutes after the White House announcement, ordered 14,214 Air Force reservists to active duty to man 24 troop carrier squadrons. Although existing tours of duty for reservists had been frozen, this was the first group called up in the Cuban crisis.

Khrushchev in an aside which was not very complimentary to Castro, reassured Mr. Kennedy that the Cuban missiles were—as Washington has always calculated—completely under Russian military control.

The serious Khrushchev note evidently was dispatched prior to a second letter, widely publicized by Soviet propaganda organs, suggesting a swap between the missile bases in Turkey and Cuba.

Kennedy Makes No Immediate Concessions on Turkey

Mr. Kennedy had rejected this out of hand, as had the Turks, saying the missiles in Turkey were part of a long-standing NATO defense arrangement designed to counter four-year-old Soviet threats and pointing out that introduction of strategic nuclear missiles into the Western Hemisphere is a totally different situation which must be solved first.

The President reiterated this in his note to Khrushchev sticking to the central theme of all U.S. statements since the crisis began Monday night with Mr. Kennedy's solemn address to the nation. This theme is that the Cuban missiles must be defused before discussions on any broader topics could be entertained.

The reducing of the Cuban missiles was left, in the first instance, to Khrushchev to undertake voluntarily; otherwise the

United States would accept U.N. observers; finally we would destroy them ourselves if need be. . . .

Khrushchev's offer to trade Cuban missile bases for Turkish, under U.N. inspection, apparently was almost wholly a propaganda gambit, however. Today and Monday the Turks are celebrating their 30th anniversary as a republic, with the shah of Iran as a state guest. These two staunch anti-Communist allies of the United States in the strategic Middle East have been a bit shaky lately, and the Soviet bid may have been designed to make them more dubious of American determination. If so, it failed.

The primary target of Khrushchev's global gamble was still Berlin [Germany] according to the best guessers here.

Time Is of the Essence

Mr. Kennedy stressed however, that there is no time to fool around in the current showdown, the gravest since Korea. He told Khrushchev he had given U.S. Ambassador [Adlai] Stevenson and other American representatives at the United Nations instructions "to permit them to work out this weekend" with their Soviet counterparts arrangements to lessen the danger of direct confrontation on the high seas.

All this assumed the Soviet leader's "good faith" in the letter which the White House would not make public. Salinger said, however, that the gist of it was evident by Mr. Kennedy's response. . . .

All that the President promised to discuss with the Soviets under Thant's auspices was "an arrangement" for a permanent solution to the Cuban problem along the lines suggested in your letter of Oct. 26 [1962].

Without the precise wording of this letter—which was a different message from the one proposing a Turkish-Cuban base trade—it was difficult on Salinger's undocumented word to say what those lines were.

There was no hint in Mr. Kennedy's reply, however, that the Turkish missile bases or any other U.S. military alliance arrangements outside the western hemisphere would be pertinent to the discussions. . . .

In releasing the Kennedy reply, the White House did not retract or modify its earlier notice that construction of the Soviet missile sites in Cuba appears to be continuing at high speed. This prospect, it has been widely hinted here, might compel the United States to take unilateral military action to knock out these sites even before the weekend was over.

Further Delays Could Increase Tensions

However, the President's message tended to calm the crisis atmosphere to some degree, although he did not specifically renounce the right to move militarily against the missile sites.

It was obvious that Khrushchev has been engaging in both public and private communications with the President, but the degree of difference between his polemic and personal positions was still not wholly clear. The White House evidently considered it significant and encouraging.

Mr. Kennedy clearly hoped for a fast answer, saying that if Khrushchev similarly instructs his U.N. spokesmen "there is no reason why we should not be able to complete these arrangements and announce them to the world within a couple of days."

In conclusion, the President again said he hoped Khrushchev would "quickly agree."

A copy of Saturday's letter was delivered to the Soviet Embassy here before being made public.

"The continuation of this threat, or a prolonging of this discussion concerning Cuba by linking these problems to the broader questions of European and world security, would surely lead to an intensification of the Cuban crisis and a grave risk to the peace of the world," Mr. Kennedy warned.

He said, however, that after Cuba was settled this country would be "quite prepared to consider with our allies" any Communist proposals for "a detente affecting NATO and the Warsaw Pact."[1]

1. The Warsaw Pact of 1955 created a military alliance between the Eastern European Soviet Bloc nations in response to the creation of the North Atlantic Treaty Organization (NATO) in 1949, which was a similar military alliance between the United States, Great Britain, and other democratic nations of Europe.

Chapter 3

Perspectives on the Crisis

Khrushchev and Kennedy Acted Cautiously to Preserve Peace

Sergei Khrushchev

During October 1962, one family member of Nikita Khrushchev had the unique perspective of watching the events of the Cuban missile crisis unfold from within the Kremlin. Sergei Khrushchev, son of the Soviet leader Nikita Khrushchev, remembers the earnest effort his father gave in seeking a peaceful solution to the crisis. In this memoir that first appeared in *American Heritage* magazine, Sergei Khrushchev discusses his father's desire to avoid an all-out nuclear confrontation. According to the younger Khrushchev, his father could have launched a full-scale nuclear attack even though the Soviet Union had fewer nuclear weapons than the United States. He credits his father's recognition that such an attack would destroy both nations as a reason for avoiding such a conflict, even at a time when the Soviet government needed Khrushchev to appear strong militarily. Sergei Khrushchev presents his father as a man who had to act brazenly for the benefit of the members of his governing body, but also one who understood the importance of not carrying the nation into a full-scale nuclear war. According to Sergei, in order to avoid public embarrassment, his father worked secretly

Sergei Khrushchev, "How My Father and President Kennedy Saved the World," *American Heritage,* October 2002, pp. 66–75.

with President Kennedy to achieve a peaceful resolution. In the final days of the crisis, Sergei states that the person to fear was not Kennedy, but Fidel Castro, who almost acted alone in order to launch missiles in a proactive strike against the United States. Sergei Khrushchev is currently a senior fellow at the Watson Institute for International Studies at Brown University in Rhode Island.

The defense of Cuba became a matter of prestige for the Soviet Union, something like West Berlin was for the United States. If you did not defend that small patch of land deep inside enemy territory that was allied to you, no one would believe in your willingness or, more important, your ability to defend your allies. That was what motivated President [John F.] Kennedy to proclaim himself a Berliner. But Kennedy had a big army in West Germany and NATO [North Atlantic Treaty Organization] at his back. How would we help Cuba if the Americans took it into their heads to attack? Send our ships and planes? The Americans would block all access to the island whether by sea or air. The only resort was to do something extraordinary enough to make Washington understand that an assault on Cuba would have dire consequences.

At the end of May 1962, Father [Nikita Khrushchev] decided to send strategic nuclear missiles to Cuba. In making this decision, he relied on our Russian and European experience—on our history. For centuries enemies had constantly replaced one another on Russia's borders: the Mongols, Swedes, Poles, Lithuanians, Turks, Napoleon, the British, Germans, and again the Germans; after the Second World War the Germans had been replaced by U.S. air bases. American bombers could demolish our cities at any moment. During its entire history Russia had been within range of hostile weaponry. Russia had to rely on sound judgment on the part of opposing political leaders, on an American President's not sending his squadrons to bomb Moscow without good reason. Father assumed that Americans—not Just the President but ordinary people—would think more or less the same way.

The Psychological Crisis of Cuba

Who would dream that Kennedy was preparing to start a war, to precipitate a Russia barely reviving after the last war into a new cycle of destruction? And for what? For the victory of communism in the United States? Father often said that communism was not a dogma but a better, richer, freer life for ordinary people. Americans were a pragmatic people. When they were convinced, sooner or later, of the advantages of the new system, they would choose it over capitalism, which was increasingly decrepit and convulsed by economic crisis. Why should we fight to achieve that goal when time was on socialism's side? And how could Americans imagine that we would attack them when they enjoyed a 9 to 1 superiority in nuclear weapons? (At the time, the CIA [Central Intelligence Agency] even thought it was 18 to 1.)

That was what Father supposed, but Americans thought otherwise. They were fortunate. For more than two centuries wide oceans had protected their land from enemies. Unlike Russians, they were used to living in security and were horrified by the possibility, however remote, of any vulnerability. The presence of Soviet ballistic missiles near America's borders evoked shock, and even psychosis. The press further inflamed emotions; the country lost its bearings; and the Cuban Missile Crisis became primarily an American psychological crisis. It seemed to Americans that they could continue to live as before only if the missiles were removed from Cuba, and removed at any price.

Nuclear War Was Imminent

Neither Father in the Kremlin nor President Kennedy in the White House was prepared for such a turn of events. They had to look for a way out of the crisis while improvising on the run. President Kennedy could not for a moment agree to the presence of missiles on the island, even though he understood that the Soviet Union would use them only in case of the most extreme necessity, just as the United States would not launch the missiles it had long before deployed in Turkey, Italy, and Britian. If he allowed them to stay, Americans would accuse him of treachery and Congress would begin the process of impeachment. The missiles must be removed, but in such a way that he did not lose control of events and unintentionally start a nuclear war.

Father felt more or less the same way. The White House was unaware of the fact that in Cuba there were not only strategic missiles but also several dozen tactical missiles, also with nuclear warheads. If America invaded, the Soviet military on the island, under the pressure of the enemy's overwhelming force and faced with the choice of surrendering or unleashing nuclear strikes on the attackers, would surely choose the latter. This was even more likely since communications with Moscow, always unreliable, would probably cease altogether at the moment of attack. With the help of tactical nuclear weapons, Soviet forces—there were 42,000 of them on the island, not the 10,000 reported by the CIA—would undoubtedly repel the invasion, destroy the landing force, and sink American ships. But what then? It was not hard to imagine how the White House would react, and it was unlikely that the world would escape a major war.

The Secret Correspondence Begins

The world was lucky. Neither President Kennedy nor Father stumbled. They resolved not to act rashly. A secret correspondence began. This had never happened before in a Cold War crisis. Previously there had been threats from both sides, reserves called up, tank treads raising dust along national borders, and diplomatic notes resembling propaganda pamphlets published in newspapers. Now serious and strictly secret negotiations were held from the first day, which could only mean that the two leaders trusted each other and believed they could agree to prevent a direct clash. Every step was weighted in this diplomatic game: Too much pressure should not be exerted, and no weakness should be revealed. Only now can we fully appreciate the caution and wisdom of the decisions taken in those days.

For instance, on Monday, October 22, Kennedy announced a quarantine of the island, virtually a naval blockade. But the next day he moved the line of interception of ships carrying military cargoes 800 miles closer to Cuba, thereby giving Father more time to react.

At first Father ordered Soviet freighters to continue forward, despite Washington's threats. After all, they were in international waters. They were accompanied by submarines, each armed with one nuclear torpedo along with conventional torpedoes. The submarines' commanders had instructions to act according to circumstances. If the ships they were guarding were attacked, they could use their weapons—even the nuclear torpedo. On the morning of October 24 no more than half an hour separated us from nuclear war.

Kennedy and Khrushchev Stand Firm

Fortunately, the time granted the Kremlin for reflection was sufficient. At literally the last moment Father decided not to take the risk; after all, missiles and nuclear warheads were already in place in Cuba. Minutes before the confrontation all Soviet transport ships carrying military cargoes were ordered to halt and turn around. But the other freighters and tankers continued on their way. Now it was time for Washington to be prudent. Kennedy also decided not to aggravate the situation, and although he knew nothing about the nuclear torpedoes, he ordered that the quarantine line be parted, first for the Soviet tanker *Bucharest* and then for a passenger ship flying the flag of the German Democratic Republic.

So each leader sent a signal to the other: We stand firm but are not taking any unnecessary risks and are ready for a reasonable compromise. However, a resolution of the crisis was still a long way off; one unsure step on either side and everything would fall to pieces.

Worry over a Planned U.S. Invasion of Cuba

On Friday, October 26, Father was brought the draft of a letter to Kennedy proposing to remove our missiles from Cuba in exchange for a guarantee that the island would not be invaded and that American missiles would be taken out of Turkey and

Italy. At almost the same moment, an intelligence message arrived reporting that America was going to invade Cuba within two days. A Soviet intelligence agent had learned this the night before from Warren Rogers, a reporter for the New York *Herald Tribune*. Rogers had been saying a noisy farewell to friends before flying to Florida, where he was assigned to cover the next day's invasion for his paper.

Father was very much alarmed. He decided not to complicate negotiations, so he deleted from the letter any mention of American missiles in Europe. The offer was now that if America pledged not to attack Cuba, the U.S.S.R. would remove its missiles from the island. The revised letter was sent to members of the Central Committee Presidium, Father made last-minute corrections by hand, and a courier took it to the U.S. embassy in Moscow. It got there just before 5:00 P.M. Moscow time—or around 10:00 in the morning Washington time—on Friday, October 26. It was quickly translated into English and sent to the Central Moscow Telegraph Office, where everything came to a halt. Technical problems piled up, one after another. The letter that might decide the fate of the world could not reach Washington for at least six hours.

Berlin Used as a Bargaining Tool

That same Friday, October 26, the KGB station chief in Washington, Aleksandr Fomin, left on his daily hunt for news. He invited a well-informed correspondent for ABC television, John Scali, to lunch in hopes of extracting something interesting from him. Scali reported the invitation to Secretary of State Dean Rusk, who in turn mentioned it to the President. Kennedy decided to bring pressure to bear on the Russians through Fomin. The man was not a big shot, but every contact had to be exploited.

Fomin has described how Scali, during the lunch, began to press him, threatening that if Moscow didn't remove its missiles, the administration would be more and more inclined to accept the military option and invade Cuba without further delay. The Pentagon, he said, was arguing that it could get rid of both the missiles and the Castro regime in 48 hours.

An indignant Fomin decided to frighten Scali in turn, without, he claims, any instructions from above. "John," he maliciously said, "you should know that . . . a landing in Cuba would untie Khrushchev's hands completely. If you attack, the Soviet Union would be free to retaliate in another part of the world. . . ."

"You're thinking about West Berlin?"

"As a countermove, it's highly probable."

That put an end to the exchange. The two finished their coffee in silence and left, Fomin to report to Ambassador Dobrynin, Scali to the White House. . . .

Father stayed in the Kremlin that night, turning restlessly on the couch in his office, half-asleep, waiting for the telephone to ring with news of trouble. But nothing happened. On Saturday morning, the twenty-seventh, he followed his usual routine, without haste or fuss. He took a shower and shaved. After breakfast he turned to official papers and saw the report of [Soviet official Georgi] Kornienko's meeting with Rogers. It vexed him. Apparently he had given way to nerves yesterday, had been too hasty when he sent the President a letter that made no mention of the American missiles in Italy and Turkey.

While Father had been dozing on his couch, President Kennedy had been very much awake—and alarmed. Scali had hurried to the White House after his meeting with Fomin and had been taken at once to Kennedy, to whom he repeated Fomin's threat. Kennedy was extremely disturbed, and by around four o'clock that afternoon Scali had already called Fomin at the Soviet embassy and asked for another meeting. The time of that second meeting is known almost precisely: minutes after 7:30 P.M. on Friday, October 26.

Scali arrived with a clearly formulated proposal: The U.S.S.R. would dismantle the missiles and remove them from Cuba under United Nations auspices; the United States would end the blockade and promise not to invade Cuba.

Fomin inquired, "Who authorized this proposal?"

"The highest authority," replied Scali.

"And what does 'the highest authority' mean?"

"John Fitzgerald Kennedy, President of the United States of America."

Fomin assured him that he would send the proposal to Moscow immediately.

If Rogers's tale of impending invasion had upset Father, Fomin's threat to attack West Berlin had unnerved Kennedy. It is noteworthy that their reactions to danger were identical. Kennedy's proposal duplicated almost word for word the conditions for resolving the crisis that Father had set forth in his letter the previous evening. That message, having been delayed at the Moscow telegraph office, began to arrive in Washington only after 6:00 P.M., Friday, October 26 (1:00 A.M., October 27 in Moscow). By then Scali had already left for his second meeting with Fomin, and Father had long been asleep. . . .

The Overlooked Meeting with Robert Kennedy

Why would he have been so obstructive? Because still another important meeting had taken place on that fifth day of the crisis, October 26. The vast official historiography of the missile crisis that has accumulated in the United States contains almost no mention of it, and Ambassador Dobrynin himself told the story publicly only once, at a Cuban Missile Crisis conference in Moscow in 1989.

President Kennedy, afraid to make a mistake and with no great faith in the Scali-Fomin connection, decided to ask his brother Robert to talk to the ambassador. The Attorney General called Dobrynin. They met at the Soviet embassy before Father's letter was read at the White House. Robert Kennedy repeated the same proposal to Ambassador Dobrynin: no attack on Cuba in exchange for the removal of the missiles. However, Dobrynin pressed him hard on the question of the Turkish missiles. Kennedy asked to make a private phone call from the next room. Upon returning, he reported: "The President said we are prepared to examine the question of Turkey. Favorably." In this situation Moscow's receiving Fomin's conflicting proposal with no mention of missiles in Europe would have complicated Dobrynin's own game. So he did not sign it but instead sent a coded message about his meeting with Robert Kennedy. . . .

The Downing of a U-2 Spy Plane Almost Ruins Negotiations

One more episode had almost irreparable consequences, and it also was due to a mutual incomprehension of the thinking on the other side. On the morning of Saturday, October 27, Capt. Rudolf Anderson took off in his U-2 for what had become a routine mission photographing Soviet missiles in Cuba. However, a great deal had changed there during the last few hours. As the U-2 was approaching the island, one of the newly constructed anti-aircraft missile batteries started the first test of its early-warning and guidance radar. Shortly after the radar was turned on, the mark of a plane at a very great altitude appeared on its screen. Only an American U-2 could fly so high.

The operators thought it must be a mistake. How was this possible? The first time you turn on the radar there's a target? Then numbers appeared on the screen: azimuth, altitude, distance, speed. There could be no doubt. They'd detected a spy plane.

The operators called the head of Soviet air defenses in Cuba, Col. Georgy Voronkov. He in turn tried to contact the commander of all Soviet forces in Cuba, Gen. Issa Pliyev, but no one knew where he was. Voronkov called again: "The target is leaving. We have two minutes left." The generals had no orders from Moscow to shoot down single American planes. They were authorized to use missiles only in case of an assault on the island, a massive bomber attack. But there was no categorical prohibition either. Now only seconds were left.

"Fire," one of Pliyev's deputies, Maj. Gen. Leonid Gabruz, breathed softly into the telephone.

"Launching," said Voronkov at the other end of the line.

Two SAM-2 anti-aircraft missiles broke from their launchers and tore into the clear blue sky. A small white puff of smoke appeared. The operator reported: "The target has been destroyed."

Informed of this incident, Father sensed that he was losing control of the situation. Today one general fires an anti-aircraft missile; tomorrow another may launch a ballistic missile. As Father said later, it was at that moment that he understood intuitively that the missiles had to be removed, that real disaster was imminent.

In the meantime, a coded message went to Cuba: "We consider that you were in a hurry to shoot down a U-2 spy plane," because an agreement on a peaceful way to deter an invasion of Cuba was already taking shape. From then on shooting down American planes without Moscow's permission was forbidden. . . .

Resolving the Crisis

So how was the crisis resolved? On Sunday, October 28, Soviet leaders gathered at 10:00 A.M. not in the Kremlin but in the government guesthouse at Novo-Ogarevo, near Moscow. Father decided that this would demonstrate our composure to the world: The Kremlin was empty, government leaders relaxing.

Father was the last to arrive. He greeted those waiting in front without his usual smile and then quickly asked his aide, "What's new?"

"There's a letter from Kennedy. During the night it was broadcast on American radio," answered an aide. "And there's something else."

"Let's go in. We'll look at everything there," said Father.

They met in a large dining room used for receiving high-ranking guests. Its long table was covered with folders in red, pink, green, and blue-gray. Each participant picked up his mail, which had been delivered by courier early that morning. Father proposed that they begin with the President's letter.

They decided to have it read aloud, even though a meticulously typed copy lay before everyone. Father's aide for international affairs, Oleg Troyanovsky, began to read in his flat, monotonous voice. It took about half an hour before he came to "Signed John Kennedy."

Glancing into a thick folder, Troyanovsky added: "We also received a report from Ambassador Dobrynin about a conversation with Robert Kennedy. Very curious."

"Read it," ordered Father.

Troyanovsky picked up some thin, transparent pages resembling cigarette papers, with a warning at the top of each against making copies, and resumed reading aloud. Father stared at him intently, listening to every word and several times asking him to repeat passages. Later, in retelling the story of how Robert Kennedy looked when he met with Dobrynin, Father would always add with a smile: "And we didn't look any better."

The President was asking for help; that was how Father interpreted Robert Kennedy's talk with our ambassador. The tone of the conversation was evidence of the fact that to delay would be fatal. "That's everything," said the aide, closing the folder.

"So, what do you think?" Father asked those seated around the table.

No one said anything. Well, Father didn't really need any advice. A clear picture was emerging. Before a war started, they had to accept Kennedy's proposal now, remove the missiles, and be satisfied with his promise not to attack Cuba. Everything indicated that the President was reaching the limit of his strength. A joint missile removal was no longer feasible. And Turkish missiles were not what counted anyway. Life was more important than prestige. Of course Father would have liked a more ceremonial assurance of the inviolability of Cuba's borders, a written agreement or decision overseen by the United Nations. But the situation was obviously too volatile. That was Father's general train of thought.

He spoke for probably about an hour, returning constantly to the premise that Kennedy's word should be trusted and that he would be in the White House for at least two—perhaps even six—more years. A great deal could be accomplished during that time. Cuba would become impregnable, wealthy, and happy. As for the Turkish missiles, forget them. Kennedy would remove them sooner or later. Robert Kennedy had confirmed that in his last talk with our ambassador and only asked not to be pressured. Father broke off and looked around at those present. Members of the Central Committee's Presidium supported its First Secretary with their usual unanimity.

While Father was persuading those present and, more important, himself, the duty officer opened the door a crack and beckoned to Troyanovsky, who slipped out of the room. When he came back, all heads turned toward him. What more could happen? No one would have risked calling the chairman's aide for anything trivial. Father broke off and encouraged him: "Speak up."

Fear of a U.S. Invasion

"We have received an intelligence report. It's been announced that President Kennedy will deliver a speech on television at 5:00 P.M.," Troyanovsky said with unusual rapidity. "The subject was not announced." It was easy to guess what it would be. On Monday, October 22, he had announced the blockade. Now, on Sunday, the twenty-eighth, the next step would be an invasion. The previous day's warnings by Robert Kennedy were being realized. The President was unable to hold out.

"At five o'clock whose time?" asked Father.

Troyanovsky only shrugged. Gen. Semyon P. Ivanov Secretary of the Defense Council, had been called to the phone at about the same time as Troyanovsky, and he replied, "Moscow time." No one knows if Ivanov just made this up, assuming that it was better to be early than late, but the general's words removed any lingering doubt. Catastrophe was only hours off.

Fear has big eyes. American television was actually reporting that the President's week-old speech of October 22 would be repeated on Sunday. We can only speculate why our Washington intelligence station turned it into a new address to the nation. Father resumed speaking. In his opinion, our agreement to remove the missiles should be broadcast at once over the radio. Father was ready to begin dictating immediately. His stenographers, who were sitting at a small table along the wall, made their preparations. But Troyanovsky had more news to impart.

"Nikita Sergeyevich, a very disturbing message has also come in from Castro." Oleg Aleksandrovich again spoke in quiet and measured tones. "The text itself is still at the Foreign Ministry, but I have written down its main points."

"Yes?" asked Father impatiently.

"Castro thinks that war will begin in the next few hours and that his source is reliable," said Troyanovsky, looking at his notes. "They don't know exactly when, possibly in 24 hours, but in no more than 72 hours. In the opinion of the Cuban leadership, the people are ready to repel imperialist aggression and would rather die than surrender." Oleg Aleksandrovich sighed, then continued: "Castro thinks that in face of an inevitable clash with the United States, the imperialists must not be allowed to deliver a strike." He looked down again at his notepad before continuing. "Allowed to be the first to deliver a nuclear strike."

"What!"

"That is what I was told," Troyanovsky responded, without visible disquiet.

"What?" said Father somewhat more calmly. "Is he proposing that we start a nuclear war? That we launch missiles from Cuba?"

"Apparently. The text will be confirmed soon, and then it will be easier to tell what Castro really has in mind."

"That is insane. We deployed missiles there to prevent an attack on the island, to save Cuba and defend socialism. But now not only is he ready to die himself, he wants to drag us with him." Whatever doubts Father might have had about his decision to remove the missiles had vanished completely. "Remove them, and as soon as possible. Before it's too late. Before something terrible happens."

The meeting's participants stared at one another incredulously. To start a world war so cavalierly! Obviously events were slipping out of control. Yesterday the Cubans had shot down a plane without permission. Today they were preparing a nuclear attack.

To general approval, Father ordered that an immediate order be sent to Pliyev through military channels: "Allow no one near the missiles. Obey no orders to launch and under no circumstances install the warheads." Father began to relax a little. Pliyev was a reliable and disciplined officer. But in the heat of battle. . . . "Remove them, and as quickly as possible," repeated Father, addressing everyone present but apparently no one in particular. Then he had sudden thought and turned to the foreign minister.

"Comrade Gromyko, we have no right to take risk. If the President announces there will be an invasion, he won't be able to reverse himself. We have to let Kennedy know that we want to help him." After a moment's pause he repeated firmly: "Yes, help. We now have a common cause, to save the world from those pushing us toward war. Send a message to Dobrynin. Ask him to meet with Robert Kennedy and advise him to wait for our answer to yesterday's letter from the President. Emphasize that the answer is a positive one."

"Right away, Nikita Sergeyevich."

Dobrynin received the coded message as the day dawned in Washington. After reading Gromyko's instructions, the ambassador at once called Robert Kennedy. They met only minutes later. Meanwhile, the conference in Novo-Ogarevo went on. Father broke a strained silence by turning to the stenographer with his usual phrase: "Let's begin, Nadezhda Petrovna."

He began to dictate. The stack of pages grew higher and higher. Finally he said: "That seems to cover everything." He made no mention of the Turkish missiles, as Kennedy had not in his letter. It was as if they didn't even exist.

At about 4:00 P.M. Moscow Radio's announcer began to read Father's letter to the President of the United States.

"Dear Mr. President, I have received your message of October 27, 1962. I express satisfaction and my gratitude for the understanding and common sense you show in exercising your responsibility to maintain world peace." The well-known announcer's voice, which had sounded somewhat shaky as he said the first few words, regained its usual resonance. "In order to quickly resolve this conflict . . . the Soviet government has ordered that these weapons . . . which you have characterized as offensive, be dismantled. We supplied them to prevent an attack on Cuba, to prevent rash actions. I regard with respect and trust the statement you made in your message of October 27, 1962, that there will be no attack, no invasion. . . . In that case, the motives which induced us to render assistance of such a kind to Cuba disappear."

The U.S. Secretary of Defense Robert McNamara has said that the first decision he took after reading the message that morning, even before consulting the President, was to cancel the surveillance flight over Cuba scheduled for 10:00 A.M. Naturally he didn't know of Castro's order to shoot down the planes, but his prudence saved everyone from harm.

A Process of Recovery Begins

Dean Rusk found Robert Kennedy at a riding stable with his children. The Attorney General listened to the news very calmly. The Secretary of State didn't realize that it was not really news to his colleague. After sending the children home, Robert Kennedy hurried to his brother. I can't say what they talked about, but the important thing is that the world survived and a process of recovery began. *Relief* would most accurately describe the mood in the White House that Sunday. Those in the Kremlin or, more precisely, in Novo-Ogarevo, felt the same way. John Kennedy decided to ignore diplomatic procedure, and he sent off his answering letter to Father before receiving the official text of the message from Moscow. It too went out over the radio. It seemed as if people in both capitals just wanted to escape from the mortal terror of the last two weeks.

So the Cuban Missile Crisis was resolved. We survived and I could write this article for the anniversary, and you can read it. But everything might have turned out differently. You, I, and all mankind might have disappeared from the face of the earth. The fact that this did not happen is the greatest achievement of those Cold War warriors President John F. Kennedy and my father, the premier of the Soviet Union, Nikita Khrushchev. Father said, more than once, "We differed from Kennedy in every respect. He defended his capitalist belief, his world, and we defended our concept of justice. We had one thing in common: Both he and I did everything we could to preserve peace on earth."

How the Crisis Strengthened America's Credibility

James N. Wallace

In the months preceding the Cuban missile crisis, the political decisions made by President John F. Kennedy, and those of his predecessor President Dwight D. Eisenhower, gave the Soviet Union the impression that the United States was not willing to follow through with a military threat. The Soviets, who had historically taken over provinces and countries in an aggressive expansion campaign, viewed any lack of follow-through by the United States in a situation where military force was required as a sign of political weakness.

James N. Wallace, journalist for the *Wall Street Journal*, suggests that recent events in Cuba and Berlin during 1961 led the Soviets to believe that they could establish a Cuban nuclear missile base with little or no resistance from the United States. Wallace argues that in April 1961, the Soviets were baffled by America's decision to overwhelm Cuba with its own military strength when a covert operation to oust Castro, known as the Bay of Pigs invasion, failed. Wallace also points out that the U.S. decision to negotiate over the right of West Berlin to remain democratic was also viewed as an unwillingness to engage in a military conflict with the Soviet Union. He concludes that the decision to act against the Soviets in an openly aggressive manner during the Cuban crisis bolstered U.S. credibility in the global community.

James N. Wallace, "Part of the Reason to Missile Showdown Was to Boost the Credibility of America," *Wall Street Journal*, vol. CLX, October 30, 1962, p. 16.

A Defense Secretary's commencement speech and a poet's talk with Premier [Nikita] Khrushchev oddly played important roles in determining that the U.S. would take the world to the brink of war to get Soviet missiles out of Cuba. For both, rightly or wrongly, raised questions about the Kremlin's assessment of America's credibility, our determination to make good on our words.

In a sense, credibility is the stuff of which modern power politics is made. Its two ingredients are power and will. In the cold war dialogue it's one thing for a Fidel Castro to bluster about Guantanamo Naval Base; unaided, he hasn't the raw force to carry through his threats. It's quite another thing for President Kennedy to say the U.S. won't tolerate offensive weapons in Cuba. The U.S. clearly had the power to remove them, but just saying so didn't prove we had the will to take the risk.

Part of the reason for the whole missile showdown blockade, diplomatic moves and preparation for invasion, was to enhance America's credibility, to prove we meant what we said about the Caribbean in hopes of making more believable our assertions about such things as Berlin.

Cuban Crisis Gives U.S. Credibility

Cuba and Berlin aren't equatable by any means, and happenings in one place don't necessarily mean similar tactics will succeed or even be tried in the other. Still, a good many people argue that if the U.S. hadn't proved its credibility in the Caribbean it wouldn't have had a whisper of a chance of being believed about Berlin.

Were there serious questions about U.S. credibility? How did they come about? And why, beyond counters for Berlin bargaining, was the Administration so concerned with correcting what it considered misreading by the Kremlin?

Without even pretending to know much about the usually mystifying thought processes of the Soviet inner circle, there are many indications the Russians thought the U.S. would back down in a truly dangerous test of will. Premier Khrushchev's entire "we will bury you" attitude reflects this. So did the building of the Berlin wall and, according to some analysts, so did the Cuba missile buildup. By this reasoning, Premier Khrushchev figured the U.S. would back down and he could get away with something President Kennedy had expressly said he would not permit. This could be an erroneous reading of the Red leader's motivations and rationalizations, but in the ICBM [Intercontinental Ballistic Missile] era it's the sort of thing that can't be ignored.

Why would the Soviets doubt America's credibility?

Part of the reason is historical. The U.S. by reputation reacts rather than acts. But seldom in modern times has the reaction come except to extreme provocation—actual, not just threatened, attacks on the U.S. And when the U.S. departs strikingly from this tradition, as in Korea, it tends to take the enemy by surprise.

U.S. Failures Provide Kremlin with False Hope

Moreover, on some important occasions the U.S. hasn't responded to a situation the way the Soviets would. Some of the most experienced followers of Kremlin affairs, for example, argue that Mr. Khrushchev was completely baffled by the U.S. failure to assure the success of the disastrous Bay of Pigs invasion. The U.S. clearly had the power to move in, even after the exile invaders had collapsed and crush Castro. In a roughly similar situation, the abortive 1956 Hungarian revolt, Moscow hadn't hesitated to impose its will with force. The failure of the U.S. to do the same thing—in an area where it had almost unchallenged physical power—left the Kremlin thinking that what was lacking in Washington wasn't the means but the will.

Ironically, many military analysts say doubts about U.S. credibility increased even while this country was building the greatest peacetime armed strength in its history. They put forward two explanations for this: Misreading of talk in high places about U.S. strategy, and the side of the build-up that was getting the most public attention.

That is why Defense Secretary [Robert] McNamara's commencement address last June at the University of Michigan created such a stir, and why there's contentious speculation about what he "really" said. It was a complicated speech, covering several important policy areas, but it became known as the "no cities" talk. Among other things, Mr. McNamara did say that even in general nuclear war the U.S. might not necessarily strike Soviet cities unless its cities were hit first. It might just aim at Soviet rocket sites and other military targets.

U.S. Unwilling to Use Nuclear Weapons

The defense chief's words could fairly be read to mean that the U.S. had such an edge in nuclear power it could absorb a first strike by the Soviets and still have an option of hitting back as it chose at military or civilian targets. But somehow in both Europe and, according to some of the experts, in the Kremlin, the whole thing was taken to indicate the U.S. had become less willing to employ nuclear weapons.

The U.S. emphasis on building up its "conventional" forces—foot soldiers, non-nuclear artillery, guerrilla warriors and the like—also apparently strengthened the idea that the U.S. was pulling back from the idea of nuclear war. In truth, the Administration was simply trying to increase its options, to build enough conventional power to hold off for a while an attack, perhaps even in Europe, while the diplomats and politicians tried to find some way to prevent the attack from escalating into nuclear war. But again, the Soviets didn't seem to understand.

By early fall, some key men in the Kennedy Administration were becoming vitally concerned about what they regarded as serious Soviet misunderstandings of U.S. intentions and U.S. determinations, in short, U.S. credibility. That's when an almost happenstance interview between poet Robert Frost and Premier Khrushchev took on major importance. Mr. Frost reported that the Soviet leader had insisted, with evident conviction, that the U.S. was too "liberal" to fight and therefore would knuckle under in future grim crises.

One result of this was much more frequent talk about U.S. willingness to use nuclear weapons. Only hours after a flying trip to Germany, Mr. McNamara called a press conference, complete with kleig lights and TV cameras, to stress that U.S.

nuclear-bomb-laden planes were standing on European runways and that we would use them, if necessary, to protect Berlin. From the White House came inspired stories that America might, under certain conditions, even strike the first nuclear blow.

Maintaining Credibility Is a Vital Element to Power

It's still considered essential to establish U.S. credibility in Soviet minds. A specific reason is Berlin, where Russia rather than the U.S. is on the short end of the supply line and has the preponderance of power close at hand. A more general reason is to reduce the danger of war by miscalculation. Historians have argued that both world wars and the Korean conflict might have been avoided if contending nations had been more aware of their foes' intentions. But awareness isn't as strong a deterrent to miscalculation as demonstrated credibility.

The U.S. apparently has dramatically demonstrated its credibility in the Caribbean. But the story is far from over.

Just because the U.S. has proved its credibility in the Caribbean doesn't mean the same tactics will produce the same result elsewhere. In Southeast Asia, as in Berlin, the logistics are almost as much against the U.S. as they are against the Communists in the Caribbean. Some key Pentagon leaders already are worrying that the apparent success of the U.S. hard line over Cuba will raise dangerous demands from the American public—and perhaps from Congress—that the same formula automatically be applied elsewhere.

Strengthened credibility will help in future crunches; it won't resolve them by itself. In all likelihood cold war credibility will be maintained only by going through some periods even more unnerving than the past few days. Says a Pentagon veteran of many a cold war crisis: "I've never been so scared as I was last week, and this time we had everything in our favor."

The Crisis Reveals the Aggressive Intentions of the Soviet Union

Barry Goldwater

By October 30, 1962, both the United States and the Soviet Union were close to finalizing a resolution to the crisis, but this outcome did not prevent Republicans in Congress from criticizing President Kennedy. Republicans claimed that in the months preceding the crisis, the Soviet Union's decision to export tanks, fighter planes, and weapons to Cuba was an act of aggression to which the United States should have responded with a naval blockade or military intervention. Republicans claimed that had the Kennedy administration been more proactive in preventing shipments of weapons into Cuba during the summer months of 1962, the crisis would surely have been avoided. Moreover, in the aftermath of the crisis, Kennedy's attempts to achieve a peaceful resolution were viewed by a more conservative group of policy makers as a sign of weakness.

Arizona senator Barry Goldwater was a staunch conservative and a strong anti-Communist who would later support American military intervention in Vietnam. Throughout the early sixties, he often criticized efforts to achieve peaceful resolutions with the Soviet Union and other Communist nations. In the following *Los Angeles Times* editorial from October 30, 1962, Goldwater argues that the Cuban missile crisis demonstrates valid reasons for the United States not to accommodate the Soviet Union in its attempts to achieve peaceful solutions to international issues. He claims that the Soviet Union historically has not pursued a policy of peaceful coexistence in its attempts to solve problems facing both nations, such as the separation of Berlin. Goldwater also contends that the United States must also abandon its "wait and see" policy and take more direct action against Communist aggression.

President Kennedy's actions in blockading offensive arms shipments to Cuba has demolished in one fell swoop many of the pet foreign policy ideas of the New Frontier [the name for Kennedy's agenda].

In the light of the situation existing today, it seems almost incredible that only a few weeks ago administration spokesmen were insisting that the Soviet arms buildup in Cuba contained no danger to the security of the United States.

At that time, of course, anyone who suggested a blockade of Cuban Leader Fidel [Castro's] Caribbean bastion was denounced as an extremist and war-monger.

No Opportunity Exists for Disarmament

But consider what the Cuban crisis of today has done to such New Frontier concepts as these:

1—The Soviet Union, under [Premier Nikita] Khrushchev, is "mellowing" in its attitude toward the West and that the time is ripe to reach a "modus vivendi" or accommodation with the Communists on outstanding problems contributing to world tension. (We know now that an outspoken enemy doesn't mellow by building offensive missile bases 90 miles from our southern coast and by compounding that aggressive act by lying to the President of the United States.)

2—Any action to counteract the Soviet Military build-up in Cuba would alternate many pro-Western countries throughout Latin America and do harm to our world prestige. (We know now that the countries of Latin America were merely

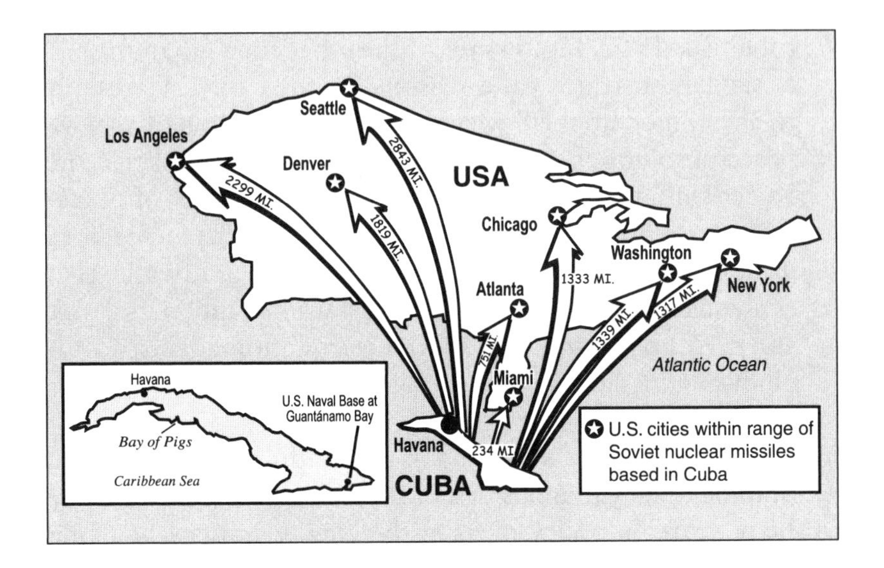

waiting for the United States to take a strong, decisive attitude toward the Communist menace in Cuba. The unanimous vote of the Organization of American States in support of the Cuban blockade was an unprecedented display of hemispheric solidarity.)

3—Now is the time to push for "a major breakthrough" on disarmament by making a series of concessions to the Soviet Union on means for control and inspection. (We know now that 1962 was perhaps the worst time in recent history to entertain serious thoughts of disarmament or to push for an agreement that placed any faith in the word of Russian leaders.)

Halting the Advance of Communism

4—The way to halt the Communist advance in the Western Hemisphere is through a grandiose foreign-aid program called the Alliance for Progress [Kennedy's 10-point program to improve living conditions in Latin America]. (We know now that even a giveaway program didn't have a chance throughout Latin America so long as Castro reigned belligerent and unmolested. Countries looking down the barrel of a Communist-controlled gun just couldn't be bothered with American talk of social and economic reform as a condition for receiving United States dollars. Consequently, the Alliance for Progress was a complete flop, which proved more embarrassing than helpful to this government.)

5—The Russians were merely going through the motions of causing trouble in Cuba to draw America's attention away from the Berlin crisis. (We know now that Khrushchev made good use of our preoccupation with Berlin to load all kinds of military weapons, material and manpower onto Cuba. We know further that the leaders of world communism are capable of applying aggressive pressure in more than one place at the same time.)

6—The military build-up in Cuba was costing the Russians so much money that they would soon tire of their adventure in the Western Hemisphere. (We know now that Khruschev regards Cuba as worthy of a price high enough to equip it with the latest, most destructive weapons in the Soviet arsenal.)

U.S. Leaders Must Not Wait to Challenge Communism

These are only a few of the erroneous assumptions that went down the drain when the President became convinced of the seriousness of the Cuban problem and switched American policy away from the costly attitude of "watchful waiting."

It can serve no good purpose today to point out that Republican leaders challenged all of these concepts during the past two years.

We can only be thankful that the government has at long last come to grips with a problem of utmost gravity and do all we can to help.

International and National Commentary on the Crisis

U.S. News & World Report

As the crisis continued, the support from the international community was generally behind the U.S. position against Cuba. International support varied widely from a desire to see proof of nuclear weapons in Cuba to war as a justified means of ending the crisis. In the following selection, *U.S. News & World Report* presents opinions from various international news agencies in order to reveal the global attitude toward U.S. handing of the crisis. Many nations expressed the opinion that in a showdown between the United States and the Soviet Union, the Soviets would be forced to back down, as a nuclear confrontation was undesirable for both sides. Support from within the United States was also varied. Many citizens felt that the U.S. tactic of an aggressive response through quarantine was long overdue. The national opinion, which was gathered through a national survey, reflected the international mood that war might be viewed as an acceptable outcome if the confrontation should escalate to that level.

Part I: International Commentary

BUENOS AIRES

South America, in the big showdown with Soviet Russia over Cuba, is lined up with U.S. leadership as seldom before in modern history.

U.S. News & World Report, "What's Being Said About the U.S. Crackdown in Cuba," vol. LIII, November 5, 1962, pp. 36–39.

Support for President Kennedy is being voiced by every government on this vast continent, by every major newspaper, and by millions of ordinary people who previously appeared apathetic or even tolerant toward Fidel Castro. Neither World War II nor any cold-war event since then had brought about such a degree of unanimity in South America.

South Americans are stunned and shocked at disclosure that the threat of nuclear warfare confronts this Hemisphere. Always before, they had considered themselves comfortably remote from atomic battlefields. Now that feeling of false security has been rudely shattered.

"Khrushchev has suffered a heavy setback," said one South American diplomat. "By overplaying his hand in Cuba, he has turned friendly neutrals into enemies and crippled the popular-front movements that the Communist parties were pushing in country after country. It may take years for the Reds to live down this blunder."

MEXICO CITY

Throughout Central America, the feeling is one of relief that the suspense of waiting for the U.S. to act is over. A statement frequently heard: "It had to be done."

If the U.S. hadn't made a stand, said one Latin-American diplomat, "we'd have been eaten up piece by piece by Communism." Said another: "It was one year too late."

The newspaper "Excelsior," of Mexico City, said on October 24 [1962] that, if war resulted, it "would be due to the madness of Fidel Castro and his destructive, irresponsible gang and the blind, insolent czars of the Kremlin."

"El Nacional," which is considered the unofficial mouthpiece of the Mexican Government, said on the same date: "The first thing it is necessary to do is to find out beyond any doubt the truth about Cuban arms—to know if they are defensive or offensive. In respect for the ideal of world peace, Cuba . . . should invite authorized organizations to make an inspection."

LONDON

Popular support in Britain for President-Kennedy's action in the Caribbean appears to be considerably stronger than most British officials and newspapers realized. A public-opinion poll showed that 58 per cent of those questioned believe that the U.S. blockade to prevent offensive missiles from going to Cuba is justified.

This public support of the U.S. is somewhat surprising in view of the position of high Government officials, upheld by leading British newspapers, that the U.S. should now be willing to make a deal with Russia. Such a deal envisions swapping Soviet missile bases in Cuba for American missile bases in Turkey or elsewhere near Soviet borders.[1]

Said the "Times" of London, which often reflects Government policy: "It is just possible, if the Cuban affair settles down to a king of long stalemate . . . that they may consider a bargain whereby each does away with a forward base or two. With a ban on nuclear testing added, the world's nerves could become steadier."

PARIS

Privately and publicly, France backs President Kennedy. President Charles de Gaulle long has advocated a firm line toward [Nikita] Khrushchev in Berlin and has been critical of Mr. Kennedy's efforts in the past to seek a compromise there.

French experts on Soviet affairs believe that, in a showdown, Khrushchev will back down. And now that the U.S. has made a show of strength over Cuba, they are more confident than ever that Khrushchev will be forced to respect American determination to maintain the West's rights in Berlin.[2]

French officials hope that the U.S. will not be forced into granting any concessions to the Russians anywhere else in the world as the price of peace.

BONN

West Germany is convinced that President Kennedy could not have acted otherwise, since Soviet rocket bases in Cuba had become a deadly danger to the United States. Chancellor Conrad Adenauer quickly emphasized that West Germany is ready to share all risks with the U.S.

1. Russian motivation for a base in Cuba is due in part to U.S. nuclear missiles along the Russian-Turkey border. 2. Russia occupies the Eastern half of Berlin while the Democratic Western half receives U.S. support.

Willy Brandt, West Berlin's mayor, called the President's decision "serious, courageous, firm and sober." Said a German industrial leader: "Finally the U.S. is willing to show her superior strength. This is the turning point."

The independent newspaper "Die Welt," wrote: "America gives notice that the time of being pushed around is over. That goes for Cuba and Berlin."

ROME

Italian reaction to President Kennedy's move is warmly sympathetic, but only up to a point. Government leaders deplore the Soviet buildup in Cuba, but do not give specific approval to the American blockade measures.

A typical comment was that voiced by the Milan newspaper "Corriere della Sera," which said: "From the strict legal point of view the decision is hard to justify. . . . But it can be justified on the basis of the elementary right of anyone . . . to defend himself from a grave and imminent danger."

TOKYO

Japanese Government leaders view the blockade as "regrettable but compelled by urgent necessity." One top official predicted that it will be effective because "the Reds always retreat before firm resolutions."

The Tokyo newspaper "Mainichi" called President Kennedy a "cool cat," but warned the United States to avoid giving the impression that it is using its vast military power against a small country.

In Southeast Asia, officials in South Vietnam, Thailand and the Philippines welcomed Mr. Kennedy's new tough line.

Part II: National Commentary

"Right thing at last," said a plant manager in San Francisco: "We're doing the right thing at last. It will be over quickly. The Russians will back down on war." An attorney in Oakland, Calif., agreed. He said: "We should have gotten even tougher with Russia. We should have told them to get out of Cuba, lock, stock and barrel, or else—not just argue about it in the United Nations."

A demonstrator pickets in Washington, D.C., after Kennedy's announcement that the Soviets were building nuclear missile silos in Cuba.

A housewife in Little Rock, Ark., said: "We wanted something like this done long before this. And now that it looks like we may get into a war, we're ready to face it."

"It is a necessary evil," said a salesman in Far Hills, N.J. "We will probably have some swap-offs with the Russians as far as our overseas bases are concerned. Each country will play a little game of chess."

A businessman in Montgomery, Ala., complained: "Kennedy should have moved a lot sooner. Even the children around here have known for a year that Castro planned offensive moves."

"Long past due." To a banker in Iowa, the U.S. action was "long past due." He added: "We are not really spiritually ready for a war, but we should have been. We should have been ready two years ago."

Another Iowan, a Des Moines housewife, said: "I've been worried about this for a long time, but I guess we all feel kind of relieved that we finally stood up and told Castro where to get off."

"I just hope this isn't politics," said an industrial consultant in San Francisco. "It's too dangerous a game for that. If we don't have better information than to be surprised in Cuba, where we should have friends, then we aren't ready for war."

And a newspaper editor in Montgomery, Ala., commented: "Kennedy is on the right track this time. I don't know too much about the legal basis of such a search. There may not be any. But this is the right time to go into Cuba and to clean it up and get it over with. I don't think the Russians will do anything about it."

This from a sales executive in Westport, Conn,: "There comes a point when a major power can't push another major power any further. I'm sure Khrushchev isn't surprised at our reaction. But it's so dangerous that I have reservations. I think we should have at least submitted the problem to the United Nations."

In New York City, a Russian-born accountant, now a U.S. citizen, said: "I'm worried. It's a rough situation. I wish we could get together with the Cubans somehow. But I can't criticize President for what he did."

"I am glad," said a Little Rock editor, "that instead of reacting to a Communist move, we've acted for a change and now can see how the Communists react to our move. There's no great alarm among the people I've talked to. They seem to be ready."

Said a gas-station attendant in Millbrae, Calif.: "It won't mean war. Did you ever force an issue on a barking dog? If you have, you know this is what happens: he turns tail and runs. The Russians always keep us off balance while they settle themselves into an area. Now we've done it to them. They'll just start trouble elsewhere."

Said a housewife in Jackson, Miss.: "I hate to say anything nice about that awful man in the White House, but I think he's right this time."

A businessman in Tallahassee, Fla., said: "What Kennedy has done is good for the country—the country's spirit and its spine. It puts us back into the American mold. We have had no leadership for years. We took insults and lies from the Russians and a petty puppet like [Fidel] Castro. Now, thank God, we are doing something about it."

A physician in Province, R.I., said: "The time has passed" for a showdown with Russia. "Even it it means war," he said, "I am in favor of the Presidents's action."

Playing with danger? In Yonkers, N.Y., a banker warned: "We are playing with dangerous stuff. There is no escape for either the smallest soldier or the biggest general if there is a nuclear war."

A law student in Berkeley, Calif.: "We have no right to tell Cuba what to do. President Kennedy admitted that. But we have no choice—right or wrong—we've too much to lose. We can only hope that we've drawn the right card."

A restaurant hostess in Detroit, with three sons of military age, said: "We can't let the Russians go on bluffing and bullying us."

A different view was voiced by a college co-ed from Port Washington, N.Y., who said: "I don't believe in nuclear testing, the arms race or military force. I believe in a different approach. We are as much to blame as the Russians. But I don't know what should be done about it."

"No choice, but—." "If we have the correct facts and the situation affects our security, the President had no choice but to take a stand," said a management engineer in Norwalk, Conn. "But I've seen a lot of decisions made incorrectly because of a lack of the correct facts."

A Florida drug salesman commented: "If President Kennedy had acted sooner, it would have been better. Most people, at least in the South, approve of acting firmly when threatened. The next move now is up to the Russians."

"This is the best time for a showdown," said a union official in Washington, D.C. "We have a good case now. The trouble with this country is that we have traded too long and negotiated too long with the Russians."

The Challenge of Castro's Cuba Remains

Time

As the crisis neared its end, the Soviet Union and the United States still had to agree on the terms of a formal resolution. Between October 26 and 28, 1962, Premier Khrushchev offered President Kennedy, through a series of secret telegrams, a commitment to the removal of the missiles from Cuba on the condition that the United States not invade Cuba. Kennedy accepted the offer in good faith on the condition that the removal of missiles would be handled by the United Nations. On October 29, acting secretary-general of the United Nations, U Thant, put together an inspection team that would oversee the dismantling of the missiles and their silos. During the course of these final negotiations, Castro tried to halt the removal and inspection of the missiles, as he felt Khrushchev should have consulted him on the matter. Eventually, with the help of the United Nations, Castro backed down and the two sides reached an agreement.

The following article dated November 9, 1962, from *Time* magazine reveals the measures Castro employed as he tried to impede the progress of the UN inspection team. *Time* also argues that, although the United States took a hard stance against the Soviet Union, Cuba remains a threat to freedom in Latin America due to Castro's efforts to spread communism.

Time, "The Nation: Foreign Relations," vol. LXXX, November 9, 1962, pp. 15–16.

After the heady experience came headachy doubts and morning-after questions.

Hardly had [Soviet premier] Nikita Khrushchev promised to back away from his Cuba missiles adventure than the Kennedy Administration started warning journalists not to get too encouraged, not to use words like "capitulation," not to assume that the "hard line," was applicable to all fronts of the cold war.

From that moment on, some of the momentum seemed to got out of the U.S.'s new drive against Soviet Communism and Castro's Cuba.

Missile Inspections Headed by United Nations

Khrushchev had not only agreed to dismantle his missiles and to remove them from Cuba; he had professed himself willing to have United Nations inspectors oversee the withdrawal. This was a basic U.S. condition. But arrangements for the inspection became confused when they were placed in the hands of the U.N. and its Acting Secretary General U Thant.

Thant organized a 19-man team to go to Cuba. At his urgent request, the U.S. obligingly lifted its blockade and aerial surveillance. Thant flew to Havana—and ran into a cold climate. Ordinarily, Fidel Castro is one of the world's most assiduous airport greeters. But he did not show up to welcome Thant, and when the two finally did meet, Castro had his gat [gun] ostentatiously holstered on his hip. In his long, rambling talks, Castro sputtered that Khrushchev had sold him down the river. As to the bargain the Russian Premier had made with Kennedy, Castro cried: "I have not once been consulted."

Castro angrily ruled out any U.N. inspection of the missiles in Cuba. He also rejected a compromise proposal that the job be done by the International Red Cross. And he ticked off five conditions that he said must be met before he would consider any sort of agreement 1) the U.S. must move out of the Guantánamo naval base, 2) end its economic blockade, 3) quit aiding "subversive activities," 4) abandon "pirate attacks," and 5) stop the "violation" of Cuba's air and sea space.

Soviet Personnel Aid in Cuban Inspections

U Thant returned from Cuba murmuring diplomatically that the talks had been "fruitful." With their strutting puppet causing an impasse, the Russians announced that Anastas Mikoyan, Khrushchev's First Deputy Premier and the U.S.S.R.'s most amiable salesman, would go to Cuba. There was an understandable notion that Mikoyan would lay down the law to Castro, ordering him to get out of the big boy's way. But on his way to Havana, Mikoyan stopped off in New York for chats at the U.N., declared that U.S. news stories about his visit to Cuba were "absolutely groundless guesses and fantasies." What was more, Mikoyan strongly endorsed Castro's preposterous propositions. The Soviet Union, said Mikoyan, "considers them just."

When Mikoyan landed in Havana, there was Castro to give him a whiskery embrace, and there were the children of Soviet embassy personnel to present bouquets to him and the Cuban leader, who held his as though it were a handful of plucked chicken feathers. The two men then disappeared into a government building to work out what Castro blandly described as "discrepancies." Mikoyan still went out of his way to praise Russia's troublesome Caribbean ally. "The Soviet people are with Cuba body and soul," he told a Cuban newspaper. "I, for my part, wish to be one more soldier of revolutionary Cuba."

Reconnaissance Shows Missiles Being Dismantled

After U Thant returned to New York, the U.S. resumed its naval blockade of Cuba. Fresh from a two-day respite in Puerto Rico, where he engaged in his favorite sport of skindiving, Vice Admiral Alfred G. Ward went back to sea to command Task Force 136. Once again, low-flying jet reconnaissance planes screeched over Cuba to photograph the state of the Soviet nuclear missiles.

The first pictures brought back of four medium-range missile sites indicated that the Russians were indeed dismantling their missiles. Some missile launchers had been removed, trailers and tents had vanished, and some areas had been plowed and bulldozed over. One picture showed a truck convoy moving away from a base.

But inspection remained the key against Communist deception. Cuban exiles and other intelligence sources were desperately warning that not all the missile equipment was being put aboard ships for return to the Soviet Union. Instead, they claimed, much of it was being stored in a long-prepared system of underground arsenals in Cuba's mountain fastnesses. To be sure, many of these sources had an ax to grind: they were embittered by the prospect of Castro's being allowed to survive, with or without Soviet missiles. But they had been startlingly accurate in their warnings of the missile buildup even before President Kennedy was convinced of it.

U.S. Should Remain Wary of Cuba

Castro's refusal to allow inspection was further proof of something that should have been explosively apparent all along: as long as he is in power, there will be a Caribbean crisis. During the agonizing days of [the] week before last, President Kennedy and Russia's Khrushchev exchanged many messages. Some of them have still to be made public, and in others there were some statements that went largely unnoticed in the U.S.'s enthusiasm over Khrushchev's backdown. Thus, Kennedy at one point declared that the U.S. would be willing to work out a deal that gave "assurances against an invasion of Cuba"—provided, of course, that, the missiles were removed and inspectors were allowed to enter Cuba.

That declaration shook a lot of people, who took it to mean that the U.S. would never invade Cuba under any circumstances. Said New York's Senator Kenneth Keating, who had been warning of the Soviet missile buildup since September. "We must be very wary about any pact which will tie our hands in preventing the spread of Communism to other countries in the Caribbean." Said a Latin American Ambassador to the U.S.: "It is to be hoped that we all do not contemplate another Bay of Pigs type failure of purpose. We are all ready to go now but tomorrow Castro may confuse or subvert some of the very governments that are the most eager to finish him off."

To reassure the worried Latin American nations, Secretary of State Dean Rusk had to call a hasty briefing of their ambassador in Washington, declared that the U.S. had no intention of underwriting Castro's future. Continuing U.S. policy, he said is to squeeze Castro to death with political and economic pressures. Moreover, Rusk explained that the "no invasion" pledge applied only to a satisfactory settlement of the missile crisis. If Castro tries to export Communism by force, the U.S. will still feel free to invade the island.

Latin America Disappointed with U.S. Stance

This assurance was less than persuasive to Latin Americans, who know all too well that Castro has been and still is trying to export Communism by subterfuge and sabotage. Just last week saboteurs, acting on Castro's orders, touched off explosions in Venezuela that damaged four key power stations in the rich oilfields along Lake Maracalbo. As if this were not enough, the Communists at week's end blew up four Venezuelan pipelines. Such acts, presumably, were the sort that President Kennedy had vowed to answer by invasion. Yet, as of last week, there was no U.S. protest or action.

While the diplomats were talking and Castro was sending out his saboteurs, the U.S. military buildup went on. Four LST troopships showed up at Fort Lauderdale, one at anchor in the channel and three nosed up to the beach with their bow doors open like yawning hippopotamuses. The 14,000 Air Force reservists that had been ordered to active duty were told that they might have to serve as long as one year. The Tactical Air Command had fighter-bombers and troop transports ready to go. The Strategic Air Command was on combat alert with a fleet of B-52 bombers carrying nuclear bombs in the air at all times.

Crisis Resolution Seen as a Success

While all this was going on, President Kennedy continued in deep consultation with his advisers, stayed mostly out of public view. At one point he did schedule a press conference—which would have been his first in seven weeks. Then he canceled it. Instead, he appeared on television for a 2½-minute speech. During that talk, he announced what had already been released by the Pentagon—that recon photos indicated the Soviets were dismantling their missiles. He said that the U.S. would agree to having the International Red Cross take over from Task Force 136 the job of stopping and inspecting Cuba-bound ships. He said that progress was being made toward the restoration of peace in the Caribbean.

At week's end, the White House stated that the U.S. would insist upon ground inspection of the Soviet missile sites in Cuba before agreeing to any settlement. But there was some talk that the Administration might be willing to have the International Red Cross do the inspecting instead of the U.N.

As the long wait went on there could still be no doubt that the U.S. Government, acting courageously and cannily had forced Russia's Khrushchev to back away from his Cuban foray. But as the days went by, there was the feeling that the U.S. might also be letting great gains for freedom slip away.

Mishaps During the Cuban Crisis Could Have Caused a Nuclear War

Alan F. Phillips

Following the Cuban missile crisis, many Americans were under the impression that the showdown between President Kennedy and Soviet premier Khrushchev was the narrowest encounter that the United States has ever had to face regarding a nuclear war. What the American public is not aware of are the false alarms that almost ignited nuclear war during this showdown. In the following selection from his article "Twenty Mishaps That Might Have Started Accidental Nuclear War," antinuclear activist Alan F. Phillips examines several occasions during the Cuban crisis that could have escalated an already tense showdown into a nuclear confrontation.

Ever since the two adversaries in the Cold War, the U.S.A. and the U.S.S.R., realized that their nuclear arsenals were sufficient to do disastrous damage to both countries at short notice, the leaders and the military commanders have thought about the possibility of a nuclear war starting without their intention or as a result of a false alarm. Increasingly elaborate accessories have been incorporated in nuclear weapons and their delivery systems to minimize the risk of unauthorized or

Alan F. Phillips, "Twenty Mishaps That Might Have Started Accidental Nuclear War," www.nuclearfiles.org, March 24, 2004.

accidental launch or detonation. A most innovative action was the establishment of the "hot line" between Washington and Moscow in 1963 to reduce the risk of misunderstanding between the supreme commanders.

Despite all precautions, the possibility of an inadvertent war due to an unpredicted sequence of events remains as a deadly threat to both countries and to the world. That is the reason I am prepared to spend the rest of my life working for abolition of nuclear weapons.

One way a war could start is a false alarm via one of the warning systems, followed by an increased level of nuclear forces readiness while the validity of the information was being checked. This action would be detected by the other side, and they would take appropriate action; detection of the response would tend to confirm the original false alarm; and so on to disaster. A similar sequence could result from an accidental nuclear explosion anywhere. The risk of such a sequence developing would be increased if it happened during a period of increased international tension.

On the American side many "false alarms" and significant accidents have been listed, ranging from trivial to very serious, during the Cold War. Probably many remain unknown to the public and the research community because of individuals' desire to avoid blame and maintain the good reputation of their unit or command. No doubt there have been as many mishaps on the Soviet side. One has been reported in which a Russian officer, on 23 September 1983, decided on his own initiative not to report an apparently grave warning on his computer screen, in the correct belief that it was a false warning. He may have saved the world, but was disgraced for failing to follow his orders; his career was ruined, and he suffered a mental breakdown. His name is Colonel Petrov, and only now in 2004 has his fine action been publicly recognized.

Working with any new system, false alarms are more likely. The rising moon was misinterpreted as a missile attack during the early days of long-range radar. A fire at a broken gas pipeline was believed to be enemy jamming by laser of a satellite's infrared sensor when those sensors were first deployed.

The risks are illustrated by the following selection of mishaps. If the people involved had exercised less caution, or if some unfortunate coincidental event had occurred, escalation to nuclear war can easily be imagined. Details of some of the events differ in different sources: where there have been disagreements, I have chosen to quote those from the carefully researched book *The Limits of Safety* by Scott D. Sagan. Sagan gives references to original sources in all instances.

The following selections represent only a fraction of the false alarms that have been reported on the American side. Many probably remain unreported, or are hidden in records that remain classified. There are likely to have been as many on the Soviet side which are even more difficult to access. . . .

August–October 1962: U2 Flights into Soviet Airspace

U2 high altitude reconnaissance flights from Alaska occasionally strayed unintentionally into Soviet airspace. One such episode occurred in August 1962. During the Cuban missile crisis on October of 1962, the U2 pilots were ordered not to fly within 100 miles of Soviet airspace.

On the night of October 26, for a reason irrelevant to the crisis, a U2 pilot was ordered to fly a new route, over the north pole, where positional checks on navigation were by sextant [a device to measure longitude and latitude] only. That night the aurora [borealis] prevented good sextant readings and the plane strayed over the Chukotski Peninsula. Soviet MIG interceptors took off with orders to shoot down the U2. The pilot contacted his U.S. command post and was ordered to fly due east towards Alaska. He ran out of fuel while still over Siberia. In response to his S.O.S., U.S. F102-A fighters were launched to escort him on his glide to Alaska, with orders to prevent the MIG's from entering U.S. airspace. The U.S. interceptor aircraft were armed with nuclear missiles. These could have been used by any one of the F102-A pilots at his own discretion.

October 24, 1962: A Soviet Satellite Explodes

On October 24, a Soviet satellite entered its own parking orbit, and shortly afterward exploded. Sir Bernard Lovell, director of the Jodrell Bank observatory wrote in 1968: "the explosion of a Russian spacecraft in orbit during the Cuban missile crisis . . . led the U.S. to believe that the USSR was launching a massive ICBM [intercontinental ballistic missile] attack." The NORAD [North American Defense] Command Post logs of the dates in question remain classified, possibly to conceal reaction to the event. Its occurrence is recorded, and U.S. space tracking stations were informed on October 31 of debris resulting from the breakup of [Soviet satellite] "62 BETA IOTA."

October 25, 1962: Intruder in Duluth

At around midnight on October 25, a guard at the Duluth [Minnesota] Sector Direction Center saw a figure climbing the security fence. He shot at it, and activated the "sabotage alarm." This automatically set off sabotage alarms at all bases in the area. At Volk Field, Wisconsin, the alarm was wrongly wired, and the klaxon [an alarm alerting pilots of a nuclear attack] sounded which ordered nuclear armed F-106A interceptors to take off. The pilots knew there would be no practice alert drills while DEFCON 3[1] was in force, and they believed World War III had started. Immediate communication with Duluth showed there was an error. By this time aircraft were starting down the runway. A car raced from command center and successfully signaled the aircraft to stop. The original intruder was a bear.

October 26, 1962: ICBM Test Launch

At Vandenberg Air Force Base, California, there was a program of routine ICBM test flights. When DEFCON 3 was ordered all the ICBM's were fitted with nuclear warheads except one Titan missile that was scheduled for a test launch later that week. That one was launched for its test, without further orders from Washington, at 4 A.M. on the 26th.

It must be assumed that Russian observers were monitoring U.S. missile activities as closely as U.S. observers were monitoring Russian and Cuban activities. They would have known

1. DEFCON stands for Defense Readiness Condition. DEFCON 5 is the peacetime level; DEFCON 1 is maximum war readiness.

of the general changeover to nuclear warheads, but not that this was only a test launch.

October 26, 1962: Unannounced Titan Missile Launch

During the Cuba crisis, some radar warning stations that were under construction and near completion, were brought into full operation as fast as possible. The planned overlap of coverage was thus not always available.

A normal test launch of a Titan-II ICBM took place in the afternoon of October 26, from Florida to the South Pacific. It caused temporary concern at Moorestown Radar site until its course could be plotted and showed no predicted impact within the United States. It was not until after this event that the potential for a serious false alarm was realized, and orders were given that radar warning sites must be notified in advance of test launches, and the countdown be relayed to them.

October 26, 1962: Malmstrom Air Force Base

When DEFCON 2 was declared on October 24, solid fuel Minuteman-1 missiles at Malmstrom Air Force Base were being prepared for full deployment. The work was accelerated to ready the missiles for operation, without waiting for the normal handover procedures and safety checks. When one silo and missile were ready on October 26 no armed guards were available to cover transport from the normal separate storage, so the launch-enabling equipment and codes were all placed in the silo. It was thus physically possible for a single operator to launch a fully armed missile at a SIOP [single integrated operational plan] target.

During the remaining period of the crisis the several missiles at Malmstrom were repeatedly put on and off alert as errors and defects were found and corrected. Fortunately no combination of errors caused or threatened an unauthorized launch, but in the extreme tension of the period the danger can be well imagined.

October 1962: NATO Readiness

It is recorded on October 22, that British Prime Minister Harold MacMillan and NATO [North Atlantic Treaty Organization]

Supreme Commander General Lauris Norstad agreed not to put NATO on alert in order to avoid provocation of the U.S.S.R. When the U.S. Joint Chiefs of Staff ordered DEFCON 3, Norstad was authorized to use his discretion in complying. Norstad did not order a NATO alert. However, several NATO subordinate commanders did order alerts to DEFCON 3 or equivalent levels of readiness at bases in West Germany, Italy, Turkey, and United Kingdom. This seems largely due to the action of General Truman Landon, CINC [Commander in Chief] U.S. Air Forces Europe, who had already started alert procedures on October 17 in anticipation of a serious crisis over Cuba.

October 1962: British Alerts

When the U.S. SAC [Strategic Air Command] went to DEFCON 2, on October 24, the British Bomber Command was carrying out an unrelated readiness exercise. On October 26, Air Marshal Cross, CINC of Bomber Command, decided to prolong the exercise because of the Cuba crisis, and later increased the alert status of British nuclear forces, so that they could launch in 15 minutes.

It seems likely that Soviet intelligence would perceive these moves as part of a coordinated plan in preparation for immediate war. They could not be expected to know that neither the British Minister of Defence nor Prime Minister MacMillan had authorized them.

It is disturbing to note how little was learned from these errors in Europe. McGeorge Bundy wrote in *Danger and Survival,* "the risk [of nuclear war] was small, given the prudence and unchallenged final control of the two leaders."

October 28, 1962: Cuban Missile Crisis: Moorestown False Alarm

Just before 9 A.M., on October 28, the Moorestown, New Jersey, radar operators informed the national command post that a nuclear attack was under way. A test tape simulating a missile launch from Cuba was being run, and simultaneously a satellite came over the horizon.

Operators became confused and reported by voice line to NORAD HQ [Headquarters] that impact was expected 18 miles west of Tampa at 9:02 A.M. The whole of NORAD was alerted, but before irrevocable action had taken place it was reported that no detonation had taken place at the predicted time, and Moorestown operators reported the reason for the false alarm.

During the incident overlapping radars that should have confirmed or disagreed were not in operation. The radar post had not received routine information of satellite passage because the facility carrying out that task had been given other work for the duration of the crisis.

October 28, 1962: False Warning Due to Satellite

At 5:26 P.M. on October 28, the Laredo radar warning site had just become operational. Operators misidentified a satellite in orbit as two possible missiles over Georgia and reported by voice line to NORAD HQ. NORAD was unable to identify that the warning came from the new station at Laredo and believed it to be from Moorestown, and therefore more reliable. Moorestown failed to intervene and contradict the false warning. By the time the CINC, NORAD had been informed, no impact had been reported and the warning was "given low credence."

1962

September 4: White House press secretary Pierre Salinger releases a press statement from President John F. Kennedy expressing concern over several recent shipments of missiles to Cuba from the Soviet Union.

September 11: The Soviet Union warns that a U.S. attack on Cuba or on Soviet ships carrying supplies to Cuba would lead to a military conflict.

September 26: The U.S. Congress passes a joint resolution giving the president the right to use military action against Cuba if the security of the United States is threatened.

October 2: In response to the continued shipment of weapons to Cuba from the Soviet Union, the United States closes its ports to any nation that continues to ship weapons into Cuba.

October 14: Fearing that Cuba will become a staging ground for offensive attacks by the Soviet Union, the U.S. Air Force uses the U-2 spy plane to conduct a series of several high-altitude reconnaissance flights over western Cuba.

October 15: Photographs taken a day earlier by U-2 spy planes reveal that the Soviet Union is building nuclear missile sites in Cuba.

October 16–22: President Kennedy and his closest advisers discuss the political and military options for removing the missiles from Cuba.

October 22: In a radio and television address to the nation, President Kennedy announces that there are nuclear missile sites in Cuba and states that the U.S. Navy will use a naval blockade in order to prevent the delivery of any more nuclear weapons to Cuba.

October 23: The Soviet Union denies the U.S. allegations of building missile silos in Cuba and accuses the United States of implementing the naval blockade in order to set the stage for an invasion of Cuba. The U.S. government begins low-altitude surveillance flights over Cuba in addition to U-2 high-altitude flights.

October 24: The U.S. naval blockade of Cuba takes effect.

October 24–25: The U.S. Navy intercepts the first Soviet tankers carrying cargo to Cuba. The ships are boarded, inspected, and released after no weapons are found on board the ships.

October 26: The Soviet Union sends a message to UN secretary-general U Thant that it has ordered its remaining merchant ships not to challenge the U.S. naval blockade.

October 26–27: President Kennedy receives two secret telegrams from Premier Nikita Khrushchev offering to remove Soviet missiles from Cuba if the United States will end the naval blockade, promise not to invade Cuba, and remove U.S. nuclear missiles from the Soviet-Turkey border.

October 27: Cuban dictator Fidel Castro, viewing the continued flights of spy planes over Cuba as an act of U.S. aggression, orders Cuban militia to shoot down any spy planes detected on radar. At noon, a U-2 spy plane is shot down over Cuba, killing the pilot; this incident is the only casualty of the crisis. President Kennedy sends a secret telegram to Premier Khrushchev offering to end the naval quarantine of Cuba in exchange for an immediate Soviet withdrawal of all missiles from Cuba. Furthermore, President Kennedy pledges not to invade Cuba.

October 28: The tension of the Cuban crisis ends when Premier Khrushchev sends a letter to President Kennedy accepting his October 27 proposal. President Kennedy wants UN inspection teams to oversee the removal of the weapons. This agreement is made without consulting Cuban authorities.

October 30: UN secretary-general U Thant arrives in Cuba to meet with Cuban officials regarding a time line for the removal of the weapons and to review procedures for the inspection teams.

November 2: Castro rejects the U.S. demand for inspection teams to oversee the removal of the weapons. Castro eventually allows the removal of the weapons under the oversight of a multinational UN inspection team. President Kennedy announces that the missile sites are being dismantled, but he insists that the U.S. government continue its anti-Cuban political and economic embargoes against the Communist country.

November 20: President Kennedy declares an end to the naval blockade.

Books

James G. Blight, *The Shattered Crystal Ball: Fear and Learning in the Cuban Missile Crisis*. Savage, MD: Rowman & Littlefield, 1990.

Dino A. Brugioni, *Eyeball to Eyeball: The Inside Story of the Cuban Missile Crisis*. New York: Random House, 1990.

Laurence Chang and Peter Kornbluth, eds., *The Cuban Missile Crisis, 1962: A National Security Archive Documents Reader*. New York: New Press, 1998.

Norman H. Finkelstein, *Thirteen Days/Ninety Miles: The Cuban Missile Crisis*. New York: Simon & Schuster, 1994.

Aleksandr Fursenko and Timothy Naftali, *One Hell of a Gamble: Khrushchev, Castro, and Kennedy, 1958–1964*. New York: W.W. Norton, 1997.

Alice L. George, *Awaiting Armageddon: How Americans Faced the Cuban Missile Crisis*. Chapel Hill: University of North Carolina Press, 2003.

Anatoli I. Gribkov and William Y. Smith, *Operation ANADYR: U.S. and Soviet Generals Recount the Cuban Missile Crisis*. Chicago: Edition Q, 1994.

Peter A. Huchthausen, *October Fury*. Hoboken, NJ: Wiley and Sons, 2002.

Robert F. Kennedy, *Thirteen Days: A Memoir of the Cuban Missile Crisis*. New York: Watts, 1969.

James A. Nathan, *Anatomy of the Cuban Missile Crisis*. Westport, CT: Greenwood, 2001.

Robert Weisbrot, *Maximum Danger: Kennedy, the Missiles, and the Crisis of American Confidence*. Chicago: Ivan R. Dee, 2001.

Web Sites

The Avalon Project, www.yale.edu/lawweb/avalon/diplomacy/forrel/cuba/cubamenu.htm. The Yale University School of Law's Avalon Project provides a series of Web pages on the most important foreign policy issues of the Kennedy administration. This link presents a comprehensive document record of the Cuban missile crisis between October 1962 and December 1963.

The Castro Speech Database, http://lanic.utexas.edu/la/cb/cuba/castro.html. This database includes speeches, interviews, and papers by Fidel Castro from 1959 to 1996. All texts are in English.

The CNN Perspective Series—Episode 10: The Cold War, www.cnn.com/SPECIALS/cold.war/episodes/10. This CNN interactive site is a companion site to the CNN history perspectives series produced in 1998. This Web site contains interviews, documents, and links to a variety of information about the Cuban crisis as well as links to other Cold War topics.

The Cold War International History Project, http://wwics.si.edu. The Cold War International History Project is a part of the Woodrow Wilson International Center for Scholars. By clicking on the Cold War International History Project link, information seekers are exposed to a variety of links, publications, and primary documents dealing with the United States and its participation in the Cold War.

CONELRAD: For All Things Atomic, www.conelrad.com. This site offers a glimpse into the Cold War culture of the 1950s and the 1960s. The site includes an overview of public-service announcements regarding safety procedures for a nuclear attack as well as an overview of the elementary school–based duck-and-cover program that taught children to hide under their desks in the event of a nuclear war.

The Khrushchev-Kennedy Exchanges, www.cs.umb.edu/jfk lib/cmc_ correspondence.html#k_to_jfk_oct23. This Web site is affiliated with the John F. Kennedy Presidential Library and Museum. This link provides access to the published versions of the top-secret telegram exchanges between Soviet premier Nikita Khrushchev and President Kennedy during the most volatile moments of the Cuban missile crisis.